ORIGINAL
CORVETTE
1953-1962

Other titles available in the *Original* series are:

Original AC Ace & Cobra
by Rinsey Mills
Original Aston Martin DB4/5/6
by Robert Edwards
Original Austin Seven
by Rinsey Mills
Original Austin-Healey (100 & 3000)
by Anders Ditlev Clausager
Original Citroën DS
by John Reynolds with Jan de Lange
Original Ferrari V8
by Keith Bluemel
Original Jaguar XK
by Philip Porter
Original Jaguar E-Type
by Philip Porter
Original Jaguar Mark I/II
by Nigel Thorley
Original Land-Rover Series I
by James Taylor
Original Mercedes SL
by Laurence Meredith
Original MG T Series
by Anders Ditlev Clausager
Original MGA
by Anders Ditlev Clausager
Original MGB
by Anders Ditlev Clausager
Original Mini Cooper and Cooper S
by John Parnell
Original Morgan
by John Worrall and Liz Turner
Original Morris Minor
by Ray Newell
Original Porsche 356
by Laurence Meredith
Original Porsche 911
by Peter Morgan
Original Sprite & Midget
by Terry Horler
Original Triumph TR
by Bill Piggott
Original Vincent
by J. Bickerstaff
Original VW Beetle
by Laurence Meredith
Original VW Bus
by Laurence Meredith

ORIGINAL
CORVETTE
1953-1962
by Tom Falconer

Photography by James Mann
Edited by Mark Hughes

To my wife Polly, and children Olivia, Daisy and Alec.

The photographs on the jacket and preliminary pages
show Corvettes from 1959 (front cover),
1954 (half-title page), 1954/1958 (title page),
1962 (contents page) and 1954 (back cover).

Published 1997 by Bay View Books Ltd
The Red House, 25-26 Bridgeland Street
Bideford, Devon EX39 2PZ, UK

Type and design by Chris Fayers & Sarah Ward

ISBN 1 870979 90 7
Printed in Hong Kong
by Paramount Printing Group

CONTENTS

THE MOTORAMA CARS

The Chevrolet Corvette is by far the most popular and successful two-seater sports car ever built. On 2nd July 1992 the millionth Corvette was assembled and sales have exceeded 20,000 every year since. Today the Corvette dominates its market, having seen off pretenders from Britain, Germany and most recently Japan. Foreign manufacturers have faced no tariff barriers or other restrictions when marketing their cars against the Corvette in the USA, but their own countries have made it difficult and expensive for the American fiberglass car to be imported to compete – and two of those countries present the further obstacle of requiring conversion to right-hand drive.

Despite this, the Corvette has outlived competition from MG, Triumph, Austin-Healey, Jaguar, Porsche, Lotus, de Lorean, Datsun/Nissan, Mitsubishi, Toyota and Honda. It is heading for its 50th anniversary early in the new millennium, with a new fifth-generation model that is clearly superior to any of its forebears and yet carries on the same family tradition of a torquey V8 in a superbly styled but practical body. Always the focused two-seater with the powerful engine and lightweight fiberglass body, the Corvette has never been permitted to dilute its image, as have its rivals, by incorporating a second row of seats.

When a federal government that had apparently not even one car enthusiast in its ranks dealt the double blow of both stringent exhaust emissions and demanding crash protection legislation, the Corvette was ingeniously adapted to pass the tests. When mid-engined sports car designs became the vogue, some prototypes with this layout were shown which were better than any of the competitors' efforts, but the superior packaging of the front-engined/rear-drive arrangement for road cars was recognized. With its ten-year-old design refined, the Corvette marched on towards its Silver Anniversary and then its highest ever

annual sales figures in 1979. Over the next 15 years the Corvette showcased brilliant engine management systems, which not only met and exceeded ever more rigorous emissions and fuel economy legislation, but also made its V8 more powerful than ever before. Between 1980 and 1990 the Corvette's maximum speed increased by 35 per cent and its high-speed fuel economy by 50 per cent.

Once it seemed that the V6 would be the big engine configuration of the future, and journalists agreed almost to a man that the V8 would never make it into the last decade of the 20th Century, yet the Corvette continues to appear with more power and economy each year. It amazed the world as the 1990s arrived with the 400bhp King of the Hill ZR1. Now the C5 or fifth-generation Corvette is with us – better handling, lighter, stiffer, faster and still one of the most beautiful two-seaters money can buy. We can even look forward to the 50th anniversary with some confidence and thank the talented enthusiasts who dreamed up the Corvette in the first place.

The extraordinary thing is that this long tradition of great sports cars has not been the product of an enthusiastic family, car-mad industrialist or motor racing dynasty. It has been made by Chevrolet, the cheap family car division of General Motors, for most of the 20th Century the world's largest corporation and one of its most profitable.

What makes this situation even more extraordinary is the fact that the Corvette has never really fitted into Chevrolet's model range. It has always been the most expensive car made by Chevrolet, usually costing half as much again as the most luxurious full-size car in the range. This has led to owners complaining that the servicing of their expensive sports cars is performed in facilities set up for the cheapest GM vehicles, and that mechanics are inexperienced in cars that are sometimes rarely seen in their service bays. In 1971,

The Corvette in its very earliest form, as introduced in mid-1953. Chevrolet's dramatic new two-seater was the first production car with a wrap-around windshield combined with reversed A-pillars.

for instance, Corvettes comprised less than 1.5 per cent of Chevrolet vehicle production.

More than once Cadillac executives have pitched the GM board with very logical proposals that the fiberglass two-seater should become a Cadillac Corvette, pointing out that it would fit in well with their expensive and exclusive range, and would be well served by the generally excellent Cadillac dealer service facilities. Corvette enthusiasts will shiver at the thought, contemplating the pointy-nosed Eldorado with wire wheels, front-wheel drive and gold chequered flag emblems that might carry the precious name today!

It is generally accepted that the Corvette lost money for its first seven years but has remained acceptably profitable since then. Though the corporation does not tolerate losses for long, Chevrolet could afford to support a loss-maker during the 1950s, particularly one that was helping convert the staid image of the division and winning high-profile sports car races with its brilliant small-block V8.

Many people were involved in the process that put a Corvette on the revolving display at the opening of the General Motors Motorama at the Waldorf Astoria Hotel in New York on 17th January 1953. Inevitably, the names of the departmental heads go into the history books, but many forgotten names were responsible for so much of the work.

Most senior of those involved was Harley Earl, a Californian who in 1927 had set up GM's Art & Colour Studio for Alfred Sloan. The GM President had realized that as the demand for cars began to be satisfied, appearance and style would become impor-

tant to buyers. Earl's team was able to define distinctive identities for each Division and interpret into metal the all-important stratifications from luxurious Cadillac to honest-value Chevrolet. Earl was alive to style and new trends – and he loved cars.

Earl was well aware of the increasing interest in European sports cars, particularly the stunning English Jaguar XK120, powered by an all-new 3.4-liter six-cylinder engine with twin overhead camshafts. While the fast-selling MGs could be dismissed as toy cars, the XK120 was a big car from a maker who also turned out big sedans. The Jaguar was also interesting because it was a mass-produced sports car, something that was not part of Detroit's repertoire. There had been big sports cars on both sides of the Atlantic before World War II, but those Stutz, Cord, Bentley, Lagonda, Mercedes, BMW and Alfa Romeo models were hand-built in small quantities for the very few who could afford them. The Jaguar could sell in quantity to an emerging post-war generation who were affluent enough to buy a car to enjoy in their leisure time. Earl had started out in the bespoke car business for wealthy clients in his Californian youth, and knew more than a little about making cars that would flatter their owners.

The XK120 was obviously the starting point for the prototype General Motors two-seater. The Jaguar had been available in roadster form since 1949, shared the 102in wheelbase adopted for the Corvette, had the same sharp definition of its cockpit area, looked good without the wire wheels that normally stated 'sports car', and apparently survived on the road with rudimentary bumpers. On this last point, the

A picture of joy to any enthusiast, and the starting point of the whole Corvette story – a 1954 chassis. With careful design and clever use of parts already in production, a dream car was turned into reality.

Comparative front views of first-generation Corvettes: model years (from top left, starting on this page) are '54, '55, '56, '57, '58, '60, '61 and '62.

Corvette's plastic body was reckoned to be tough enough to withstand normal parking knocks anyway, though it would be best not to try nudge-parking against a collector's '53 today. The bumpers eventually fitted were more decorative than practical, with only the front bumperettes solidly mounted to the frame.

The proposed GM sports car started with a considerable advantage over the Jaguar because it had no need to carry the old-world symbolism of a vertical radiator grille. And though the Corvette was of comparable length and wheelbase, its track was a full 6in wider.

Earl had a talented team to call on to put together his ideas. Traditionally the head of Styling takes the credit for his department's work; in the corporate world his job is the one on the line if his staff do not perform, and the creative people are happy to be anonymous. Memories grow dim, but recently published research by Noland Adams has identified names not previously associated with the Corvette. Henry Lauve had been with GM Styling since 1939 and was probably the principal stylist of the prototype. Semi-pontoon fenders with high-mounted, recessed headlamps and a bulbous fin finishing the rear were his trademark. Lauve had also been deeply involved with the development of the wrap-around windshield of the fabulous 1951 Le Sabre dream car, and the new Corvette would be the first production car with this dramatic feature. Carl Renner, who had

joined GM in 1945, was a master of the toothy air intake grille, and his designs were adopted for both the Corvette and the 1953 full-size Chevrolets; he would also go on to originate the side coves for the '56 Corvette. Others who worked on the early stages of the project were engineer Robert F. McLean in particular, as well as body engineer Vincent Kaplan Sr and draftsman Carl Peebles.

To confuse competitors who might hear of it in Detroit's close automotive community, Earl's baby was called 'Project Opel', a name that suggested that this car was destined for General Motors' subsidiary in West Germany. McLean is credited with the basic layout of the design, and is said to have schemed it by starting at the back and working forwards. After placing the bucket seats as far back as possible, he sketched in the steering wheel and instrument panel, and then positioned the motor as close as could be behind this panel, and low to the ground. Front wheel position followed from installing the standard front suspension cross-member in front of the motor, thereby establishing the 102in wheelbase. This approach also ensured that here was a true sports car layout with the engine and transmission well back in the frame, and a low center of gravity. Do we blame MacLean for the Corvette's inadequate leg room? No, this problem should have been picked up by other members of the design team. But if you buy your 501s with a 34in or longer leg, do not expect to be

comfortable for long behind the wheel of a straight-axle 'Vette.

A full-size plaster model of 'Project Opel' was complete by June 1952, and during this process the design was shown to newly appointed Chevrolet Chief Engineer Ed Cole. He was overwhelmingly enthusiastic about the as-yet unnamed roadster and wanted it for his Chevrolet division. At this point, of course, it could still have become a Cadillac, and collected a race-proven V8. But Cole was by this time deeply involved in the development of the Chevrolet division's new small-block V8 and must have foreseen that this compact unit would be the ideal power plant.

Cole had himself been the driving force in finishing the new Cadillac V8, his first project when he was appointed Chief Engineer of the Clarke Avenue luxury car division in 1947, after a career that had started there in 1929. The new 1949 overhead-valve Cadillac V8 displaced 331cu in, was compact, lightweight and oversquare, and used the latest casting techniques in its manufacture.

From Cadillac, Cole brought with him engineer Harry Barr, who had been largely responsible for the 331 and would be key to the success of the new small-block Chevrolet. With one successful V8 to their credit, what better time to get on with designing another? These two were used to doing their engineering the Cadillac way: quality, refinement and the pursuit of excellence were part of the heritage they

brought with them. Along with other dedicated engineers and designers, they would do so much to transform Chevrolet from GM's boring utility car line to the premium American performance car brand for most of the second half of the 20th Century, without losing its sales lead.

Once the plaster mock-up was approved by GM President Harlow Curtice and Chevrolet General Manager Thomas H. Keating, the task of making it all work passed to Maurice Olley, who headed Research and Development. His role was to design a chassis using as many production parts as possible, and to make the new car handle as well as it looked.

Olley was an Englishman who had arrived in the US as a supervising engineer with Rolls-Royce of America in Springfield, Massachusetts. When this operation closed with the onset of the depression in 1930, Cadillac chief engineer E.W. Seaholm hired Olley to work on suspension systems to improve the ride and handling of the Cadillac range.

Olley discovered that the pitching that had been the curse of luxury cars until this time could be cured by giving the front suspension a longer period than the rear, and devised his coil spring and unequal wishbone system to achieve this by giving the front wheels twice the movement of the rear. This was the system now universally known as an SLA, which is often incorrectly taken to be an acronym for 'Short Long Arm'. Olley has stated that the derivation is more

interesting than this, and dates back to research he was doing in 1931. Initially the suspension was developed for an experimental project known as 'Stream-Lined A', and the initials stuck to the coil and wishbone system thereafter. In early guise the system used a lever type damper as its top link, but by 1949 this had become a plain wishbone and the damping was by a Delco double-acting telescopic unit, mounted inside the coil spring. Part of Olley's team's achievement was to use a threaded bush in each pivot to give precise location, and this too was carried on into the Corvette's front suspension. The sway bar was also developed by the same team to control roll, the initial problem with independent front suspension.

This system was first used on the 1934 Cadillac, Oldsmobile and Buick, and was later adopted by Pontiac and Chevrolet after they had briefly used the complex Dubonnet independent front suspension system instead. And, of course, it was later copied by the rest of the industry world-wide. Seaholm later described Olley as a genius for his work in this field and he went on to head GM's R&D department until his retirement in 1955. He is also the man who invented the now indispensable words 'understeer' and 'oversteer'.

When Olley penned the widely published initial sketch for the Corvette chassis and layout, he was not just drawing the conventional, but was the master of the subject expressing the best that could be done

with what was available at the time. His achievement for the Corvette was to get it right immediately; exactly the same chassis with only improved rear axle location went on to an outstanding eighth place at Le Mans in 1960, and numerous other race wins and championships over the ten-year period from 1953.

Olley was able to provide the prototype with handling and road-holding that was unlike any American car of the time, by using this corporate front suspension assembly, a radiator inclined rearward, a steering column that was almost horizontal by prevailing standards, and a rear axle mounted onto thoughtfully located semi-elliptic multi-leaf springs – and by tying the components together with a fully boxed and diagonally braced frame.

By now officially a Chevrolet and rapidly becoming a running reality, the new sports car had to be given a suitable name. Many names had been considered and rejected when Myron Scott, a Chevrolet public relations executive, heard of the board's decision that the car's name should begin with the letter C. He claimed that he looked through a dictionary and quickly found Corvette. He liked the sound of the word and its association with a fast and agile naval vessel. When he submitted the suggestion to Ed Cole, who had by now adopted the car as his own, the Chevrolet Corvette was born as a brand.

The prototype had to be finished for display at the opening 1953 venue of the now traditional General

Comparative rear views of first-generation Corvettes: model years (from top left, starting on this page) are '54, '55, '56, '57, '58, '60, '61 and '62.

Motors Motorama. It was to be shown as a fully working and driveable car, and all the work required to achieve this had to be done in the six months remaining before this deadline.

Having adopted Harley Earl's sports car, Ed Cole was now obliged to use the only performance engine that Chevrolet had – the 235.5cu in straight-six. This was an uprated version of the 216.5 offered only as an automatic. It was logical to build the show car as an automatic – Chevrolet's Powerglide was one of the best in the industry – and, as any hot-rodder knows, it is much easier to build a one-off car if you can dispense with the complication of a clutch pedal.

The hood kept its low line by the use of triple side-draft carburetors, a header tank for the low-mounted radiator was mounted along the left side of the engine valve cover, and the water pump was modified to mount lower. By careful tuning the engine was able to make 150bhp.

At this stage there was no doubt that the Corvette was intended to be a steel-bodied car – glass-reinforced plastic was used simply as an expedient to get a prototype finished in time for the Motorama. However, extensive experimental work had been carried out with fiberglass as a body material, and a 1952 Chevrolet convertible in this material had completed more than 13,000 miles when it was rolled over. It came to rest on its wheels with the driver unhurt, and with less body damage than might have

been expected with steel. This convincing – but unplanned – demonstration of the strength of the new material certainly opened more than a few eyes to its potential, not least because this car was 200lbs lighter than its steel-bodied sister.

After molds had been made for the new prototype Corvette, which was finished on 22nd December 1952, bodies for a further two cars were produced, to be finished with less urgency. One was used as a test vehicle or 'mule' by both Styling and Engineering, and the other was completed as a second Motorama car for a series of small shows in Canada later in the fall of 1953. The second car was distinguished only by its lack of cowl scoops, which would not be seen again until the 1956-57 model.

The reception of the Corvette was tremendous and Chevrolet, who need never have revealed that the body was made of plastic, made the most of the publicity that the new material generated as the Motorama Show moved from city to city. The day after the opening of the show in New York, GM President Harlow Curtice announced that the new sports car would go into production in June. At the end of March 1953, after wavering between steel and fiberglass, the decision was finally made to go with the latter and to establish a production line capable of building 10,000 cars per year.

No-one knew then that it would take until 1960 to achieve that production target…

1953–1955

The first Corvette rolled off the short Flint assembly line on 30th June 1953, just over five months after EX-122 had been unveiled at the New York GM Motorama. This was a genuinely saleable mass-produced sports car and certainly the most advanced – and even futuristic – car produced in any American assembly plant on that summer day. It was destined to become an icon for millions of Americans, most of whom had yet to be born on this Tuesday in June.

This Polo White Corvette with Sportsman Red interior was almost identical to the Motorama car. It was driven off the end of the line with its top down and hubcaps on by Tony Clabber, a foreman at the plant who would later move the 550 miles west to St Louis, Missouri, to continue to build the new Chevrolet sports car when production moved there at the end of the year. The top was stowed in the well behind the seats perhaps because a photographer was there to record the event. Normally the top would be up and wrapped to protect the canvas fabric, so that after a test drive, tune-up and rectification of any faults the car could be shipped to the Chevrolet dealer that had ordered it.

The Flint assembly operation was a pilot plant in the true sense. The work stations had particularly skilled operators, who were expected to refine the production process, develop the many special and ingenious tools, gauges and fitments which are part of any production line, and establish the best order and timing for each assembly process. In particular the bonded assembly of the fiberglass body – an entirely

new process for mass production – had to be proven to be practical on a moving assembly line, and techniques had to be devised to make sure that every bonded body would fit and look exactly right.

This first Corvette production operation was in a disused customer delivery building on Van Slyke Road on the south side of Flint, some 50 miles north of Detroit. It was described at the time as having a production line the length of only six chassis, and the total staff including management was about 75.

Then, as now, Flint was an industrial city dominated by GM and the manufacture of automotive components. All the skills and equipment necessary to productionize a new car were available locally, and the engineers and designers responsible for the car were only an hour or so south. It is clear, however, that there was never any intention to make this city the permanent home of the Corvette: even before the first car was produced, plans were afoot to set up a volume production plant in St Louis, Missouri, where production of some 50 cars per day was anticipated. The Flint cars were produced at the rate of about three per day and only 300 had been finished by Christmas 1953. Subsequently this building became part of GM Assembly Research Center, where pilot studies were done on future models – effectively the task performed there for the first Corvette.

Though a few more Corvettes were built at St Louis before the turn of the year, mass production there started in earnest in early 1954, with key staff who had moved from Flint to use their pilot line experience on a full-scale moving assembly line.

The first 300 Corvettes were hand-built during the second half of 1953. This is number 006, completed within days of the first car. Styling was futuristic, assisted by the absence of big bumpers which were thought unnecessary on a plastic-bodied car. On the Motorama car there had been a 'Corvette' script between the nose emblem and the front grille, but the production car looked better without it.

A '54 model (opposite), with no differences in side view from the '53 other than different hubcaps. Windshield was dramatically raked on early Corvettes, but became a little more upright from '56. All Corvettes were Polo White until 1954, in which year an estimated 12 per cent of cars were painted Pennant Blue, Black or Sportsman Red, like this one. Long exhausts, introduced mid-1954, were first influence on Corvette of future Chief Engineer Zora Arkus-Duntov. All '53 and '54 Corvettes were delivered on whitewall tires, with a change to tubeless in '54.

Convertible top for '54 was beige canvas, replacing the black of the first year of production. It had only two intermediate bows, giving an angular profile which contrasted with the sleek appearance with the top down and folded out of sight. Side vision was restricted for tall drivers.

The 1955 model was externally identical to the '54, apart from the all-important gold 'V' imposed on the Chevrolet emblem to indicate the presence of the new small-block V8 motor. A very few six-cylinder cars were also built in '55. Smooth appearance was enhanced by lack of door handles, but did not impress potential buyers who expected them – and lockable doors – on a car which cost only a few hundred dollars short of a Cadillac.

Some of these staff were returning home because they had originally come from Missouri to study and develop the production procedures.

Located at Natural Bridge Avenue and Union Boulevard, the St Louis plant had been assembling Chevrolets since February 1920. The Corvette operation was moved into the Fisher Mill building, a multi-level structure originally constructed for the manufacture of wooden car body parts. The Corvette was always going to be a limited production vehicle, and, unlike other Chevrolet products that were assembled in a number of plants across North America, it made sense to locate the new fiberglass car in a city that was central to its market in terms of population. The intention was to build 10,000 cars per year, and all the machinery was in place to achieve that number.

The '54 models built at St Louis looked very little different to their predecessors. Externally the only obvious changes were the new convertible top (in beige instead of black) and longer exhaust tailpipe extensions (incorporating deflectors to direct exhaust gas to the road). Polo White was still the most popular color, and still striking in age when an all-white car was quite unusual. About 3200 cars were built in Polo

White for the model year, but additionally there were 300 '54s in Pennant Blue, 100 in Sportsman Red and four in Black; Pennant Blue cars came with Beige interiors, but otherwise the trim color was always Red.

The longer tailpipes on the exhaust were the first evidence of Zora Arkus-Duntov's influence on the Corvette. Born in Belgium in 1909 of Russian parents and raised in Russia, he graduated with a degree in engineering from Leningrad University, and went on to work on a number of automotive projects in Germany and Belgium before arriving in New York in 1940. With his brother Yuri he opened a machine shop there and was involved in various military projects during the war years.

Prior to his involvement with the Corvette, Arkus-Duntov is particularly remembered for his Ardun overhead-valve aluminum cylinder head conversion for the flathead Ford V8. These were used by the English Allard sports car company, for whom he went to work and sometimes race until 1952. Sydney Allard had finished third in the 1950 Le Mans 24-hour race in one of his J2 models, fitted with a V8 Cadillac motor. His co-driver was American Tom Cole and Cad-Allards became very popular as budget clubman racers in the US.

Duntov's practical can-do background and racing experience (he had also raced Porsches in Europe) were exactly what Chevrolet needed to get its uncertain sports car licked into shape. By 1954 he had been hired by the Division and almost immediately got himself involved with the Corvette. He did not stop at experimenting with exhaust outlets but went on to become Chief Engineer and the single most important figure in the first 20 years of the car's history.

Though the Corvette assembly area at the large St Louis plant had been set up to put together 50 cars a day, this target was not achieved before it was noticed that this sensational new plastic-bodied wonder was not selling as well as expected, and that an embarrassing number of unsold cars were accumulating both at the Missouri factory and around the country. In July 1954 there was a temporary cutback to 300 cars per month, and this reduction became permanent. By the end of 1954 only 3640 cars had been built and more than a quarter of them remained unsold. Note that the model year end still came in December at this stage: it was not until 1956 that the new year's models were launched in October.

The stylists were hard at work on the new body for 1956 by the time the original-shape car was given the V8 engine that it deserved. Only about 625 '55s with

this engine were built, making this model one of the rarest (and expensive) of all Corvettes – but it would still be just as desirable even if ten times that number had been built. Externally, only a gold V superimposed on the V of Chevrolet on each front fender showed that the V8 was installed, while the serial number (on the plate on the driver's door hinge pillar) gained a V prefix; not until 1972 would it again be possible to identify a Corvette engine from the chassis number.

There were still possibly 800 unsold '54s in Chevrolet's inventory by the time '55 production started, and Chevrolet's own records show that about 140 of these were not sold until 1956. It is likely that production of the 'six' continued to help boost sales of the '54s so that they could at least claim to be identical to the current model.

Other changes for 1955 were few, but extra colors were offered for the body, interior and top. No records survive, but new colors are known to have included Corvette Copper, Gypsy Red and Harvest Gold, the last teamed with a dark green convertible top, a yellow interior and yellow wheels. Whereas all wheels had until now been painted red, those on Corvette Copper cars also differed, being Bronze. A white vinyl soft-top was also introduced, previewing a change to this material in 1956.

Wheels on Gypsy Red '55s were matched to body color, while all other paint choices had contrasting wheels. The '55 V8 is one of the most valuable and sought-after of all Corvettes.

DIMENSIONS

Length	167.25in
Width	69.8in
Height	51.5in
Wheelbase	102.
Max track	59in
Curb weight	2850lbs

Headlamp of 7in diameter concealed behind mesh grille successfully transferred glamorous race car imagery to the 1953-55 Corvette; 'bucket' was painted matt black. Striking rear lamp pods were separately molded and bonded to the body before filling and painting.

BODY & TRIM

Comparing the front of the 1953 production model with the Motorama car, the Corvette script was missing below the round crossed flags emblem, resulting in a cleaner frontal appearance. Behind the front wheel, a practical chrome strip now extended along the door to the rear wheel opening to protect the body sides. This strip ran below the Chevrolet script on the front fender with an upward and forward pointing flash, whereas the shorter version on the Motorama car had been above the script with the flash facing down and rearward. This strip was lowered for a good engineering reason: it now covered a major seam where the upper body was riveted and bonded to the lower sill panel in front of and behind the door.

Another improvement was the loss from the top rear of the front fenders of small scoops, which had always looked a little fussy. The two earliest cars also lacked outside rear-view mirrors, but 003 certainly had one. More surprising was the lack of outside door handles, which made for a smooth body line but would infuriate luxury car buyers who would not want to fumble in the rain to open a wet side window to enter their unlockable Corvettes.

The convertible top was hardly seen, or omitted, on the Motorama cars, but this was essential equipment on a production car. Needing to be simple and light to operate for easy folding into the limited storage compartment, it used only two intermediate bows which gave a rather angular appearance when erected. The ingenious lifting rear bow allowed the top to be fully hidden when stowed, a system that became a Corvette tradition and was not copied by others for some 30 years. To prevent chafing of the folded top, the bottom of the compartment was lined with felt and 'footman' straps were provided to secure the top. Tops were initially made of a canvas material, black for '53 or beige for '54. For '55 vinyl was phased in on white tops, beige continued in either material, and dark green was used on Harvest Gold cars only.

While there have been times when standards have dropped, particularly in the late 1970s, the general quality of the Corvette's fiberglass bodywork has been superb, and almost always superior to the output of those European manufacturers who use the material because it is so well suited to low-volume manufacture. Most European enthusiasts would expect to be able to identify a fiberglass-bodied car because of its uneven surface, wavy panels and distorted reflections, and are often amazed to discover that all Corvettes are fiberglass. This is because the bodies of all Old World cars were until recently laid up by hand into a female mold and left to cure naturally. There would be little control over thickness and the reverse side of each panel was at best uneven and at worst hairy with exposed matting. The uneven thickness ultimately showed on the external surfaces as well.

Most of the panels in the majority of the Flint '53 Corvettes were hand-laid, but using the 'vacuum bag' variation of this method. This process used atmospheric pressure to compress the uncured panel. A sheet of clear plastic film, the bag, was placed on the wet inside surface of the panel, and a vacuum pump was used to suck air from beneath it. This not only made the panel stronger, but the smooth plastic gave the panel a better underside appearance.

GM technicians would not tolerate such methods for long. Advised by Robert S. Morrison, whose Molded Fiberglass Company of Ashtabula, Ohio, manufactured all the early Corvette body panels, they devised a better way of making fiberglass panels by forming them under pressure between matched metal dies. During the 1953-62 period, this two-stage process worked in the following way.

Fiberglass thread was fed into a chopping machine and blown out of a tube against a rotating pre-form screen. This consisted of a very fine fiberglass mat which was fixed to a former held at a convenient working angle. The chopped threads adhered to the screen because the operator used a hand-held gun to simultaneously spray resin and hardener to hold the pre-formed panel together and build up its thickness. Rotating the work ensured that the chopped fibers were laid in all directions, making the final panel stronger as a result.

The pre-form, now like a bulky mass of matting, was run through a continuous oven to semi-cure the resin, and then placed in the bottom half of the matched dies. A second layer of fine matt was now placed on the top and a measured amount of resin poured on to the pre-form. The operator then closed the metal dies together under great pressure, while they were heated by internal electrical or hot water coils. It should be noted that a gel coat is not used in this process, the high molding pressure ensuring that the panel is uniformly dense and the outside fine mat enabling release. E.J. Premo's 1954 Society of Automotive Engineers Paper *The Corvette Plastic Body* describes these fascinating processes in detail.

After about three minutes the dies were reopened and the cured panel was removed from them with the

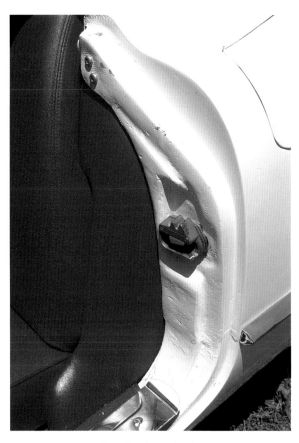

Many everyday details of the design were well thought out and effective. The step plate was stainless steel and the door striker plate was bolted through to a substantial steel reinforcement. Fresh air vent was operated by under-dash lever, and was waterproof when closed. Other design aspects were not quite so successful. Windowed compartment for rear license plate was novel, but stole trunk space and suffered condensation. With little fall in the filler pipe, right turns with a full gas tank often led to fuel spillage and odor.

characteristic perfect finish on both sides. Final trimming of the edges was all that was required before the panels could be shipped. The advantage of this two-stage process was that from the very beginning the Corvette never had a bad reputation for fiberglass problems, and never suffered from porosity, starring, delamination, osmosis or any of the other woes familiar to owners of those other cars with hand-laid bodies.

The body production process developed the previous year at Flint was interesting. The body was bonded together from its 62 component parts on the second floor of the building, which was outdated even then. It was built up stage by stage starting with the underbody – the largest single component. This was the last piece to be converted from vacuum bag production to matched die in early 1954; thereafter all panels were made by the Molded Fiberglass Body Company. Panels arrived at the plant neatly nested together, having been designed this way to save expense in both transport and storage, and to reduce damage on the journey.

The underbody was scuffed where it was to be bonded, necessary holes were drilled using fixtures for precise location, and steel reinforcements were riveted and bonded into place for the seat mountings and also beneath the foot boards at the base of the firewall. The English term for firewall is 'bulkhead', and this word is certainly more appropriate to the Corvette because this panel, being of a flammable material, will be consumed by fire rather than resist it! Bare Corvette fiberglass is not easy to ignite, but once painted it will

Early exhaust tailpipe was short and said to allow fumes to be drawn back into passenger compartment, so a longer version appeared in mid-1954. Trunk lid during 1953-55 incorporated molded-in mesh radio antenna to take advantage of the non-conductivity of fiberglass.

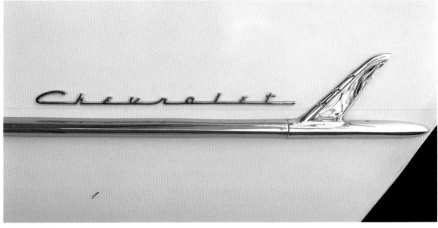

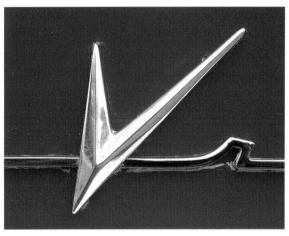

Side scripts said 'Chevrolet' – the word 'Corvette' appeared only on the small nose emblem and the horn push. Gold anodized 'V' superimposed over that letter in 'Chevrolet' indicated presence of the 265cu in V8 for '55.

light very easily and when burned out only a matted mass of loose fiber remains.

The underbody panel was then mounted right way up onto a trolley or 'buck' to which fixtures could be attached for exact location of the remaining body panels. Each buck was pulled through each assembly station by a conveyor chain in the floor.

To bond the panels, a fast-setting resin adhesive was manually squeezed from paper cones similar to cake frosters. These were filled with resin and hardener, the mixture becoming hot as it started to cure. Panels were generally butt-jointed with the adhesive squeezed into the joints. Then a thin fiberglass

bonding strip was bonded behind the joint to give it strength. Specific fixtures and clamps were used to locate the panels prior to and during bonding to ensure accuracy. Rivets were also used in the important connections, for instance between the upper rear body panel and the underbody.

Additional steel reinforcements were riveted and bonded into the body, in particular in the door hinge and lock pillars, beneath the dash top and behind the seats. The most important was the cross-braced radiator support which was bolted between the inner fenders. This not only supplied a stress-free mounting for the canted-back radiator, but also stiffened the front inner and outer fenders – it was essential that these should not shake because they are forever in the driver's field of vision.

The panels still required extensive rubbing down before paint could be applied, and skilled labor was essential to finish the bonded panels prior to painting. Stage by stage the body was gradually completed and was then steam-cleaned for final surface preparation. To remove all moisture and to complete the curing of the bonded joints, the finished body was left in an oven for an hour at 140° Fahrenheit. It then received its first coat of sprayed-on primer, which was dried in another oven. The oven tended to reveal very small holes in the bonded and filled panel joints.

After more filling and hand/power sanding, the body was primed again, sanded smooth again, and finally spray-painted in its final color, still mounted on its trolley. Masks were used to allow painting of the

COLORS

1953					
Body	**Wheels**	**Soft-top**	**Interior**	**Dash top**	**Dash lower**
Polo White	Red	Black	Red	Red	White

1954					
Body	**Wheels**	**Soft-top**	**Interior**	**Dash top**	**Dash lower**
Polo White	Red	Beige	Red	Red	White
Pennant Blue	Red	Beige	Beige	Blue	Beige
Sportsman Red	Red	Beige	Red	Red	White
Black	Red	Beige	Red	Red	White

1955					
Body (code)	**Wheels**	**Soft-top**	**Interior**	**Dash top**	**Dash lower**
Polo White (567)	Red	White/Beige	Red	Red	White
Pennant Blue (570)	Red	Beige	Dark Beige	Copper	Beige
Corvette Copper (573)	Bronze	White	Dark Beige	Copper	Beige
Gypsy Red (596)	Red	White/Beige	Light Beige	Gypsy Red	Beige
Harvest Gold (632)	Yellow	Dark Green	Yellow	Woodland Green	Harvest Gold

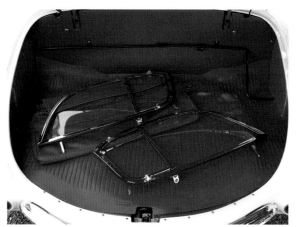

A relic from another era, the side windows when installed made toll payment and hand signals difficult. Side windows were stored in the trunk in a bag. For '54 the bag fastened to the front of the trunk compartment.

Convertible top was neatly stored beneath hinged deck lid, released by button on seat divider. Detail shows socket for rear soft-top bow in deck lid.

trunk area in the appropriate color and the engine compartment in black. Because Corvette engine compartments have never been body color, it has always been easy for an owner to change the paint finish of a car – and difficult for later owners to discover the original factory-applied color. Corvettes of the 1953-62 period did not carry paint code identification plates.

When painting was completed, and the body lightly baked, buffed and polished, paint flaws were remedied and the body was ready for trimming. This meant fitting not only the dash, seats and carpets, but all other body components including the steering column, fuel tank, lamps and electrical system, as well as the raised convertible top and the bumpers, which were mounted to the body rather than the chassis frame. Even the detachable side windows (known as side curtains) were installed before the body was dropped onto the chassis.

When all chassis components, battery and exhaust system had been added, four whitewall tires on red-painted wheels were fitted and the car was allowed to roll for the first time. The last job on the rolling chassis was on-car balancing of the front wheels, Chevrolet claiming this as an industry first for a production line.

Almost the final job was the body drop, when the fully finished body was lowered onto the running chassis and the 11 mounting bolts fastened. There were two at the outer ends of the rear cross-member, eight with shorter bolts around the passenger compartment to mount the underbody panel, and one at the center of the radiator support frame to carry the front end.

Once the electrical connections had been made, exhaust tailpipes fitted and brake, accelerator and transmission controls connected, the car was filled with coolant and a gallon of gasoline ready for a final check. It was started and driven off the end of the line, then taken for a leak test in a water spray booth and road-tested around the limited parking area behind the factory. After rectification of any faults, the finished Corvette was finally parked outside to await dispatch to the selling dealer.

Changes to the body to accommodate the V8 for 1955 were few. The design of the hood panel had to alter to clear the now centrally mounted air cleaner of the V8, the X reinforcement being replaced by a simple cross rib. Externally, of course, there was that all-important golden V superimposed on the V of Chevrolet on each front fender.

CHASSIS

Corvette production has always been an assembly process, with components delivered from all over the 48 states and Canada. The frame came into the plant already built by the A.O. Smith Corporation, which would later also build whole bodies for the next generation of Corvettes in the 1964-67 period. It

CHASSIS NUMBERS

1953	E53F001001 – E53F001300
1954	E54S001001 – E54S004640
1955	E55S001001 – VE55S001700

Fiberglass contrasts on driver's door posts. Early finish from vacuum-bag molding process was charmingly crude in unobtrusive areas (white car), but matched-die technique – progressively introduced in late '53 through early '54 – gave much better results (red car). Switch is for courtesy lamps, on which GM was mean-minded: they were standard equipment in '53, an obligatory option for '54-55, a genuine option for '56-61, and standard again thereafter! Frame number plates identify the sixth car built in '53 and a V8-powered '55 with V-prefix – not until 1972 would it again be possible to identify engine type from the frame number.

resembled the contemporary Chevrolet passenger car frame but its wheelbase was reduced by 13in, from 115in to 102in. It featured fully boxed side rails and diagonal I-section cross-bracing to add rigidity. There was a substantial rear cross-member, but the front was closed only by the front suspension subframe.

The front suspension subframe was made up from heavy gauge pressings. This was a standard Chevrolet production part, in use on passenger cars since 1949. The whole assembly was extremely strong, resistant both to accident damage and to rust, in spite of being protected by only a thin coat of semi-gloss black paint. Whereas the same subframe was welded into passenger cars, future generations of restorers would be grateful for the decision to use bolts and nuts to secure it in the Corvette. The rails were arched at the rear to allow for the rear axle's movement. This frame continued with only detail changes for the ten years of production of this first Corvette model.

This chassis frame design was typical of the era and it is interesting to note that its diagonal cross-bracing precluded lowering either the seats or the footwells.

This led directly to two criticisms of the design. First, the seats were too high, which was uncomfortable for tall drivers, particularly with the top up. Second, the driver's feet were too high up for long-distance comfort. Both of these problems would be addressed on the next generations, which dispensed with the diagonal bracing – said to weigh 213lbs – but unfortunately lost torsional rigidity as well.

From the start of production until mid-1954, the frame number of the car was stamped in two places – at the center of the left rear diagonal cross-member and on top of the left frame rail approximately below the gas filler. Thereafter until the end of production it was on top of the left frame rail, beneath the center of the driver's door.

The chassis frame, which was delivered to the assembly plant already painted black, started down the line upside-down. Rear springs and pre-assembled rear axle (complete with hubs) were fitted first, then the front suspension and steering (already fitted to the cross-member) were installed. The frame was then inverted and the engine and transmission, which had already been tested, were dropped onto their mounts and fastened in place.

INTERIOR

In contrast to competing sports cars of the time, the seats were generously proportioned to fit the widest drivers. Unfortunately there was not matching leg room for the tallest, a problem that would remain on Corvettes for the next 43 years. Steel frames supported the vinyl-covered sprung cushions, the driver's adjustable on runners, the passenger's fixed. Seats remained unchanged for the first three years of production apart from a mid-1954 modification to the back cushion to accommodate the revised

convertible top folding mechanism. Seats were always color-coordinated to the interior, with 13 rows of stitching on the center panels of each cushion.

Detachable side curtains instead of glass windows had one advantage: they freed up the space normally taken by the window regulators and allowed extra arm room and useful door pockets, just like the British Mini six years later. The pleated theme of the seats was continued on the upper part of the door panels and forward on the kick panels.

All '53s were white with red interiors. The seat divider was an extension of the external body and white-painted surfaces continued inside the car on the lower dash and the full-length door pull. The white lower dash treatment continued when other colors followed in 1954, except when the interior was beige or yellow, and remained through 1957.

Carpet was a close-pile material called Rox Point and matched the seat color. It was tailored to the floor shape and the seams were bound.

INSTRUMENTS & CONTROLS

The major dial in front of the driver was the speedometer, contained in a nacelle which matched one on the passenger's side housing the radio loudspeaker. Reading to 140mph, the speedometer needle, driven by cable from the transmission, did not describe a true arc. Markings in kilometers were never made available: Canada did not adopt the metric system until 1971 and European sales of the Corvette were negligible.

A tachometer was an innovation in an American car and this unit, mounted in the dash center, also incorporated a total engine revolution counter, called a totalizer, to monitor engine life. This sensible device

All '53 Corvettes and most '54s teamed red interiors with white bodywork. These shots are actually of two different cars, a '53 (opposite above) and a '54 (opposite below), but there are no significant differences. The chromium-plated rail of the windshield was continued back to encircle the cockpit before plunging down between the seats, a styling trick made possible by the hidden but easily raised convertible top. Seats were wide but leg room was not generous.

Detachable side windows meant no window regulators or channels in the doors, leaving the space saved for useful door pockets and extra elbow room.

Door panel on Gypsy Red '55 was mainly white vinyl with red stitching, though this interior color was nominally Light Beige.

Dash on '55 model shows the simple layout with central tachometer and matching quadrants for speedometer and radio speaker. Compared with earlier cars shown on page 23, note different colors for steering wheel and carpets. The '54 was the first year for Conelrad national defense emergency markings on the self-seeking radio dial; if you saw a mushroom cloud in the sky you tuned to 640 or 1240 kilocycles AM for further instructions. Tachometer on a '54 shows useful total engine revolution counter; logically this would have been a better guide for service intervals than the usual mileage-based recommendation. Brake and accelerator pedals are seen with cold air vent control in foreground. Steering wheel was passenger car unit with special horn button emblem; crossed Chevrolet and checkered flag logo, still used on Corvettes, was devised for the Motorama, after an earlier design with the Stars and Stripes as the left-hand flag was rejected.

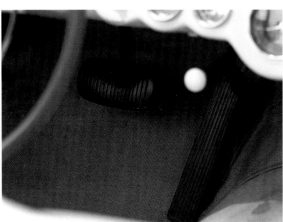

was cable-driven by the ignition distributor. Minor instruments were ranged either side across the dash, the fuel and coolant temperature gauges to the left, ammeter oil pressure and impulse-wound clock to the right.

The wide brake pedal was top-hung and worked a single master cylinder stamped 5454480. There was no servo assistance, and, with brakes borrowed from the heavier full-size cars, none was required. The parking brake emerged from under the left side of the dash, released by a twist of the handle. Built into the speedometer bezel was a parking brake warning light, which glowed red if the under dash lever was not fully released when the ignition was turned on.

The hard rubber accelerator pedal pivoted on the floor, acting on a top-hung lever to operate the complex linkage for the three carburetors.

The Powerglide shift lever was on the transmission tunnel, an unusual location at a time when the steering column shift was universal, but essential to emphasize the sporty image. The shift pattern, embossed on the top of the white plastic shift knob, was R-L-D-N-P, and requires concentration when driven by a modern driver for the first time.

The 1955 introduction of three-speed manual transmission necessitated a clutch pedal. This was pivoted concentrically with the brake pedal and operated the clutch mechanically. Like the automatic shifter, the manual shift was bolted directly to the transmission with the lever moving in a boot on the tunnel. The bezel which retained the boot was embossed with the manual shift pattern.

At first the windshield washers on '53 cars were operated by a floor-mounted foot pump, but in mid-production this was changed to a vacuum-powered system with a push button to the left of the steering wheel, next to the control for the lights in the traditional American position. The '54 models continued with this system, but for '55 a floor-mounted pump was used once again, but this time with an additional cable to cycle the wiper switch while the washers were in use.

The heater/fan control knob and choke were to the left of the radio, the cigarette lighter to the right. Just below either end of the dash were initially two hood release knobs, but this arrangement was replaced by a single knob during 1954. The headlight dimmer switch was to the left of the brake pedal.

ENGINES

Chevrolet did not have a V8 in 1953 and had not offered one for more than 30 years. Their staple had been the economical and unexciting overhead-valve in-line six, launched in 1929. This had proved to be just the right kind of engine for the depression years, the various sixes selling more than 25 million units by 1953. This was the engine generally known as the Stovebolt Six. The great rival, Ford, had their V8 for most of this time; it may have been a flathead but it had prestige.

Chevrolet's 235.5cu in Blue Flame six had been an option with automatic transmission only since 1951, the 216.5 having been supplied when standard shift was ordered. In 1953 the smaller capacity was dropped and the 235.5 was made available in two versions – 108bhp with the three-speed manual gearbox or 115bhp when combined with Chevrolet's own two-speed automatic Powerglide.

The six-cylinder Chevrolet engine was slightly under-square with a bore of 3⁹⁄₁₆in and a stroke of 3¹⁵⁄₁₆in. Firing order was 1-5-3-6-2-4. Interestingly, 1953 was the first year in which Chevrolet used aluminum pistons, 8.0:1 in this application. Designed for rugged service, the engine gave maximum torque of 223lb ft at only 2400rpm. The single low camshaft was gear-driven at the right side of the engine where it also drove the fuel pump by a cam and the distributor by a bevel gear. Long pushrods opened the slightly offset valves via cast rockers which pivoted on a common shaft.

To make the Blue Flame six go like a sports car engine should, its output was improved by classic tuning methods to give an extra 35bhp at 4200rpm. The modifications included a high-lift camshaft to improve engine breathing and stronger valve springs with solid valve lifters to allow higher revs without valve bounce. The valve train was concealed by a special valve cover which was lowered at the front end to allow hood clearance. These engines were initially supplied by the Tonawanda, New York, engine plant, but in 1954 supply was taken over by the Flint engine plant and Tonawanda-built units would not again grace Corvette engine bays until the 1965 model with the optional 396cu in MkIV big-block.

To take advantage of premium fuel, the compression ratio was increased from 7.5:1 to 8.0:1. Hood clearance also dictated that side-draft carburetors be used. When installed in the Bel Air, a single-barrel down-draft Rochester or Carter was fitted. The solution to maximise performance was to fit triple side-draft YH Carters, initially with part number 2066S and later 2066SA. Thus was born the first Tri-Power, although the title was not coined until the mid-1960s and it was applied to a progressive linkage system. The original aluminum intake manifold had no cast number, though service replacements carried the number 3707064. The aluminum intake manifold was painted blue-green to match the engine.

Unlike the Motorama car, the production '53 lacked air cleaners but instead there were three bullet-shaped air intakes – closed-end intake extensions with a metal gauze to keep out insects and gravel. With side-draft carburetors which were prone to flooding when hot starting, extensions were also useful in that they carried excess fuel away from the hot exhaust.

In mid-1954 an air cleaner system was introduced which used a ducting fabricated of sheet metal press-

ings, to link the three carburetors to two steel-meshed air cleaners topped with chrome-plated lids. A mesh-covered outlet was incorporated into the underside of the duct between the two cleaners to drain away any fuel from flooding carburetors.

Fuel was supplied by an elaborate AC double-acting fuel pump (part number 5592675). Incorporating a top sight glass, this unit not only pumped gas to the triple carburetors, but also supplied extra vacuum for the atmospheric windshield wiper motor, to boost its performance when the throttle was open and therefore vacuum was low.

Engine breathing was further enhanced with a dual exhaust system with a dual-outlet cast-iron exhaust manifold (cast with the number 3836108). The forward pipe swept under the motor to the right side of the car and then back through the holes in the chassis cross-brace. The rearward pipe went up the left side of the car. Mufflers were oval reverse-flow type, mounted ahead of the rear axle and angled upward to clear it.

Earlier 1953 cylinder blocks were cast 3701481, but after mid-October the cast number changed to 3835911 and this block was used to the end of

Corvette six-cylinder production in 1955. The block number can be seen by removing the fuel pump. All six-cylinder motors were painted the then standard Chevrolet blue-green.

The cylinder head was cast number 3836066 for 1953 only. The valve cover was retained by two domed nuts and gasket washers screwed onto studs centrally mounted into the head. For 1954 this was changed to a more oil-tight arrangement of four bolts around the perimeter of the cover, the cast number of the head changing to 3836241.

The valve cover carried on the right side white decals bearing the words 'Blue Flame' with an arrow and red speed lines. The word 'Special' with a stylized lightning flash on the left side of the cover appeared on the '53 only. In '54 it was replaced by a '150' in an outline arrow, on the right front of the valve cover. Some '54 cars were fitted with chromed valve covers with no decals. The white-on-blue engine top graphics looked superb, more dramatic than any that would follow in the next 45 years of production. But then the V8 engines that followed actually performed and, unlike the lethargic six, they needed no boost from a graphic designer.

The 235cu in Chevrolet straight-six seen in a '53. Triple side-draft Carter YH carburetors mounted on an aluminum intake manifold boosted power to 150bhp at 4500rpm.

Right side of '53 six shows chromium-plated coolant header tank, plain for this year only. Below it is full shielding for ignition system, to reduce radio interference. This early car has foot-operated windshield washers; after car number 175 washers were vacuum-powered.

The low hood line of the Corvette combined with the height of the six-cylinder motor required the use of a separate coolant header tank. This was made of chromium-plated brass and was attached to the right side of the engine directly above the ignition shielding, in contrast to the Motorama cars, where it was mounted on the left side. In very early 1954 this smooth-finish tank was replaced by one with two band-shaped depressions pressed into it. The pressure cap was chromium-plated and stamped '778' and '#4', which indicated that the system pressure was 4lbs. The radiator was made of copper by the Harrison company, with a plate stamped 3130953, and was painted gloss black. The length of the six-cylinder motor was such that the engine-driven fan was close enough to the radiator core that no fan shroud was required. The water pump, cast 3706011, was specific to the Corvette and not shared with other Chevrolets.

It will be easily deduced from the foregoing that the Corvette was a car waiting for an engine – and it was given that engine in 1955. Whenever the Corvette is compared with other sports cars, two key features stand out over 40 years – and these are the features that have made it the best-selling two-seat sports car ever. They are the durable double die-molded fiberglass body, and the torquey, powerful and simple V8 motor.

This does not mean that the six-cylinder cars of 1953 and '54 are not interesting: they are fascinating to study and represent the root stock from which the line grew. The six was the only motor available to Harley Earl, Ed Cole and the rest, and indeed without it there would be no Corvette as we know it.

The six is not without its charms. To anyone raised on V8s, it is impressively long and tall under the fiber-glass hood. Very careful building can reduce internal friction and stress with rewarding results. Adjusting and synchronizing the triple carburetors so that they will run under all engine temperature conditions is a challenge to the most experienced enthusiast and can defeat the best in the hobby. Once the six is running well it makes a smooth sound all of its own through the dual exhaust system. But the overwhelming rightness of the small-block V8 available in the '55 Corvette makes the sixes pale in comparison.

Those who thought the six too slow or dull were rewarded in January 1955 with the announcement of the optional 265cu in V8. The effect was dramatic.

Suddenly the Corvette was transformed from an interesting looking fiberglass-bodied two-seater – but one that was a disappointment to drive – into a true sports car, a car with all the power you dare use under the right foot and a little bit extra as well.

Sports cars have to be about driver satisfaction. They either need to be light, or if, like the Corvette, they are quite heavy, then they need a motor that has sufficient power to make them feel light. The new 265 V8 had power to spare: 40bhp more than the 155bhp of the six, and 35lb ft more torque at 3000rpm. The V8 felt livelier too. Whereas the stroke of the six was ⅟₁₆in short of 4in, the V8's stroke was only 3in. Combined with larger piston area, that meant instant response and higher revs. This was reflected in the tachometer markings: the six read to 5000rpm, the V8 to 6000. Neither engine was rev-limited by the pump-up effect of hydraulic lifters, which were not used on the Corvette until 1957.

The new engine was also lighter than the six, reflected in the shipping weight of 2665lbs for the V8 against 2695lbs for the six. The engine itself was 40lbs lighter, other equipment adding the extra 10lbs. Gear ratios and final drive were unchanged, but the V8 adopted the appropriate torque converter for its bolt pattern.

The new V8 was introduced simultaneously in Chevrolet's 1955 passenger car line, rated at 162bhp with a Rochester two-barrel carburetor and single exhaust, or 180bhp in the Power-pack version with a four-barrel and dual exhaust. The Corvette shared major components with the Power-pack version, but was rated 15bhp higher due to the use of a high-lift camshaft (cast number 3711355) with 20 per cent more lift. Interestingly, the lift of this cam is actually higher than that of the legendary Duntov cam.

Installed, the 265 small-block was lower and its center of gravity was further back. Although it had two more cylinders, it was considerably shorter, the crankshaft being only 24.73in long. While the six was supported at the sides of its block, the eight used a steel hoop sandwiched between the water pump and the block to carry the engine weight to the rubber mounts on the frame rail brackets, which were also relocated. The frame itself was modified to accommodate the shorter but wider motor by the simple expedient of notching the right-hand rail to accommodate the fuel pump – it was that easy.

Early '54 motors had the same bullet-style air cleaners as the '53, but halfway through production a more effective dual-pan air cleaner would be introduced. The word 'Special' was omitted from the valve cover.

Right side of '54 engine shows coolant header tank with twin bands. Ignition shielding was sometimes chromium-plated, as was valve cover; either is correct, and the chromed valve cover had no decals. All 1954 windshield washers were vacuum-operated.

Triple Carter YH series carburetors were never easy to synchronize.

The carburetor for the V8 was initially a Carter 2218S WCFB (the initials stand for Wrought Cast Four Barrel). This had an automatic choke and a progressive throttle that opened the front pair of butterflies before the rear. Later in 1955 this was replaced by a Carter 2351S with a simplified linkage and no vacuum link to the distributor, which was also changed. The intake manifold was a cast iron unit identical to that used on the passenger cars and carried the cast number 3711348. Like the block, it was painted orange-red (all sixes had been painted blue-green).

As on all small-block Chevrolets, the cylinder heads (cast number 3703523) were identical and interchangeable side to side. Intake and exhaust valves were a conservative 1.72in and 1.50in in diameter. Valve covers were the same stamped steel with Chevrolet script as on the passenger cars, but for this application they were chromium-plated.

The cast iron cylinder block carried the cast number 3703524 on the driver's side rear top face adjacent to the transmission bellhousing. All small-block V8s carry their cast number at this location, and this must be considered the second most important number on any Corvette. To anyone interested in any model of Chevrolet, this number tells a great deal

about a car's history, or lack of it – indeed checking these numbers can become a compulsion! Further verification can be gleaned from the casting date represented as month-day-year, the last as a single figure if the source of the block, correctly for a Corvette, is from Flint. These numbers are unlikely to be faked, though they can be. A dental technician would find it easy to place a correct cast number onto an incorrect block...

The 265cu in 3703254 block was the only one produced by Chevrolet for 1955 and it was used in all V8 car and truck applications. It had no cast-in boss for an oil filter – indeed the '55 Corvette had no oil filter at all. Some passenger cars had an external oil filter mounted in front of the right-hand cylinder head, but this was not used on the Corvette, which therefore relied on regular oil changes to keep its moving parts in good order.

The 265 motor used a forged crankshaft with a 3.00in stroke. The five main bearing journals had a 2.30in diameter, and big end or rod journals 2.00in. This crank would also interchange into the 283

motor through 1961. Cast numbers could be found on the outside of webs 1, 2 and 5, and were respectively 3815822, 3834627 and 3836266.

Most of the books concerned with restoration and originality completely fail to mention the crankshaft, perhaps not a surprising omission given the emphasis placed on static judging when cars meet to be assessed against each other – the crankshaft is after all invisible in a finished car. In his excellent series *Chevrolet by the Numbers*, Alan L. Colvin tackles this much neglected subject in full, including the essential cast numbers, and the owner seeking to build a truly correct car must refer to the appropriate volume of this work, which also covers correct connecting rods, pistons and camshafts.

The crankshaft is the essence of a Chevrolet V8 and a beautiful piece of sculpture in its own right; nothing looks nicer than one freshly ground and polished by the machine shop. Proper balancing with the connecting rods and pistons also helps to achieve the smoothness and tractability which so impressed all who tried this motor back in 1955.

Glorious small-block 265 V8 introduced in '55 gave Corvette the power it needed. Also fitted to full-size Chevrolets the same year as an option, it would become the most successful car engine of the second half of the century. Steering column was painted interior color for its whole length.

V8 was a better fit than the six in the engine compartment, but a fan shroud was required because the engine was shorter than the six.

Small-block cranks are either forged steel or cast nodular iron. The former, used in all 1955-62 Corvette V8s, are stronger and more expensive to build, and generally associated with high-performance engines. The cast nodular iron cranks were produced from 1964, using the same casting numbers, and will retro-fit into the earliest V8s. The different types can be identified by looking at the parting line

of the casting on the flywheel flange at the back of the motor. On the cast crank this line is narrow and quite sharply pronounced, while on the forged steel crank it is ¼in to ½in wide with no sharp edge.

Forged steel connecting rods carried no numbers, measured 5.70in center to center, and used a pressed-in pin; rod bolts were of ¹¹⁄₃₂in diameter. The pistons were tin-plated cast aluminum, flat-topped with no valve reliefs, giving a compression ratio of 8.0:1.

The camshaft fitted to the '55 V8 had lift of 0.404 (intake) and 0.413 (exhaust), and carried the cast number 3711355. As well as its 16 lobes, it had an eccentric at the front to drive the fuel pump via a pushrod, and a bevel gear at the rear for the ignition distributor.

Exhaust manifolds were cast iron, unique to the year and shared with other models; cast numbers were 3704791 (left) and 370492 (right). While cast numbers are not part numbers, they adhere to the same convention – odd numbers left and even numbers right. The very few exceptions to this rule with Corvettes are usually caused by the application

ENGINE IDENTIFICATION

Engine block cast numbers

Year	Engine	Cast number
1953	235cu in (six)	3701481 (early), 3835911 (late)
1954	235cu in (six)	3835911
1955	235cu in (six)	3835911
	265cu in (V8)	3703524

Stamped engine number suffixes

Year	Engine	Suffix	Rating
1953	235cu in (six)	LAY	150bhp auto
1954	235cu in (six)	YG	150bhp auto
1955	235cu in (six)	YG	155bhp auto
	265cu in (V8)	FG	195bhp auto
	265cu in (V8)	GR	195bhp manual

of a popular part in a differently handed way, such as electric window motors. Parts not fitted to a car in pairs can have part numbers that are odd or even. This odd and even parts number convention is extremely useful when sorting through used parts at a swap meet, and when checking GM boxed parts.

Surprisingly, many experienced Chevrolet countermen are unaware of this system. Even some of the major aftermarket Corvette parts specialists, who re-number all parts to their own codes, ignore this very sensible convention. A very large number of wrongly supplied parts are simply the right part in the wrong hand, and GM adopted this system to avoid this problem. One cannot leave this subject without throwing a brick at the replacement door glass industry, which unfortunately uses a parts numbering system impressively known as the National Automotive Glass Specification (NAGS). Their part numbers use odd or even for left or right entirely at random, yet door glasses are always handed!

On arrival from Flint, the V8 engines were fitted with their triple carburetors, throttle linkage, fuel pumps and electrical ancillaries, and then bolted to their Powerglide transmissions. The engines were test run on three dynamometers, the mixtures and throttle openings synchronized, valve lash adjusted while running and the transmission tested under load.

ELECTRICS

The six-volt ignition system on the six-cylinder cars used a Delco-Remy distributor stamped with the model number 1112314 on the breaker plate together with manufacture date. The unit incorporated an adjustable graduated octane selector with its vacuum advance unit to compensate for variations in fuel with the tuned engine. The distributor also included a tachometer cable drive unit.

The coil was an 115394 unit embossed with the figures '394', and the spark plugs were Delco 44-5. The negative ground battery was a Delco 15AA6-W, with 15 plates. The Delco generator, stamped 1102793, was mounted low on the left side of the engine and had a 5in diameter pulley, while the 45-amp voltage regulator was mounted on the firewall.

The starter motor was a Delco 1107109. In 1953 Chevrolet introduced across its model range the modern system of starting the engine by a further turn of the key beyond the ignition position, instead of by a separate starter button, so the Corvette was the first new Chevrolet with this feature designed in. During February 1954 an improved and more powerful starter motor (1108035) with four field coils replaced the first motor, which had only two.

Because the body was fiberglass and lacked a steel firewall, the ignition system had to be surrounded by pressed steel shielding. AM radio signals are particularly prone to interference, so shielding would be incorporated into all radio-equipped Corvettes until

Four details from 1955 V8 compartment: air cleaner removed (top) to show Carter four-barrel carburetor and fuel filter; individually shielded distributor and plug leads (left), now with 12-volt electrics for V8 cars; front-mounted hinge design (above) means awkward adjustment for good hood fit, replaced by plain hinge for '58; pipes and shut-off valve (below left) for '55 pattern of heater, which recirculated cabin air only.

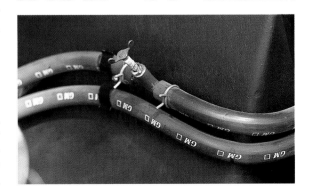

1982, by which time radio design had improved so much that shielding was no longer required. Normally the shielding on 1953-55 models was painted the same blue-green as the engine, but some '54 cars have either the top, bottom or sometimes both parts of the shield chromium-plated; the wing and domed nuts securing the shielding were also chromium-plated. Of all the original components on the car, over the years none would be discarded more quickly than the shielding, and few of those owners who decided to junk it would have had any idea of its intended function!

All Corvettes had rear-mounted radio antennae to reduce ignition interference, but maybe an additional reason was that they look neat back there. On 1953-55 models the antenna was incorporated into the trunk lid to emphasize the possibilities of the new wonder body material.

With the introduction of the V8 came a change from six to 12 volts, along with the new electrical equipment that this required. For continuing six-cylinder production, however, six-volt electrics were retained. Thus the production line had to build cars of similar appearance in two voltages.

The 12-volt generator of the V8 was marked 1102025 and incorporated a drive gear for the tachometer, since the 1110847 distributor now fitted had no facility for a tachometer drive. This distributor had a vacuum advance, superseded later in the year when it was replaced by the 1110855, which had centrifugal advance only. An attractive 1955-only chromium-plated canister and lid surrounded the distributor, the coil had a chromium-plated cover, and all the plug wires were sleeved with metal braid and grounded at both ends.

The vacuum-powered wiper motor was replaced in the V8 by an electrical unit, still driving via a cable and pulleys, and turned on and off by a frail cable-operated switch. The battery tray was larger to take the negative ground Delco 25M50-W 12-volt battery (now with nine plates), but this tray was also used in the few 1955 sixes.

TRANSMISSION

The only transmission available for the 1953 and '54 Corvette was the Powerglide two-speed automatic, a simple and reliable design which remained an option until 1969. During that time it was developed to handle the torque of the mighty big-blocks, and was adapted to become a leading drag racing unit.

The early Powerglide, introduced by Chevrolet in 1950, had a cast iron case of modular construction, built up from four castings. Gear ratios in low and reverse were 1.82:1. It had a transmission fluid capacity of 11 US quarts and there was no fluid cooler. The cases carried two different identification codes in this period – LV for '53 and C for '54-55.

Listed as basic equipment for the '55 model was a

Shift lever for the Powerglide automatic in a '54. Sequence is completely different from today's P-R-N-D-L and requires concentration.

three-speed Saginaw manual gearbox, but it did not become available until late in the year and only about 75 cars, all V8s, were built with it. Like the heater and radio, automatic transmission was a compulsory $178.35 option for almost everyone. Although not a distinguished 'box, the iron-cased Saginaw would continue to be listed as basic equipment every year through 1969, with minor modifications.

The Saginaw 'box was specially adapted to the Corvette because it had three threaded bosses in its tail housing to accept linkage for a floor shift. Other cars using this 'box had steering column shifts, essential with the three-abreast bench seats of the era, and had no need to attach any part of the shifter to the tail housing. The main case was cast 3845122 and the tail housing 3722946. A shaped stainless steel escutcheon was stamped with the positions R-1-2-3, and located the rubber shifter seal and boot. The shift lever was angled backward and topped by a white plastic ball.

The clutch was a single-plate, three-lever unit of 10in diameter, operated by mechanical linkage with over-center spring assistance.

The rear axle was a modified version of the standard Chevrolet unit with a 3.55:1 ratio, or 3.27:1 as an option with manual transmission. It was driven by what now appears to us as a conventional drive shaft, but which was known then as a Hotchkiss drive. Other Chevrolets at that time used an enclosed torque tube, which located the axle well but made it pivot about the end of the gearbox. This would not have worked with the inclined rear spring, and the open drive also had the potential to transmit rather more power.

The drive shaft was cleverly arranged so that it did not interfere with the diagonal cross-bracing of the chassis, but was carried over the top of it. Universal joint failure at speed could have had a catastrophic effect on the driver or passenger with a transmission tunnel of fiberglass, so a safety loop was thoughtfully provided to surround the front of the drive shaft.

The axles were coded as follows: LW (early '53), MW (late '53 and '54), AE ('55 Powerglide), AH ('55 three-speed 3.55) or AD ('55 three-speed 3.27). These codes can be found at the front of the right axle tube, near the carrier housing.

First few '53s were fitted with Chevrolet Bel Air domed hubcaps (far left) before vented production design (left) arrived for all '53-55 models; all '53-54 wheels were painted red. Wheel opening edge flare recalls the original intention to build the Corvette body of steel.

WHEELS & TIRES

All 1953-62 Corvettes used a 15in × 5K pressed steel wheel with five-stud fixing. Wheels on the '53 were plain but the '54 and '55 wheels had three unused lugs, which were intended to retain the hubcap when these wheels were used on full-size Chevrolet cars.

Regardless of body color, '53 and '54 wheels were dip-painted Sportsman Red. On '55 models the wheels were color-coordinated to the exterior finish by spray painting. To prevent road grit and gravel entering the full wheel covers and rattling inside, the four gaps between the rim and wheel center were filled with rubber seals on '55 models.

Three different wheel covers were used in early production in '53, the third design being adopted through '55. The first '53 cars left the Flint line wearing plain domed hubcaps, which were the Full Wheel Discs offered as an optional extra for the '53 Bel Air. In the rush to meet the June production date specified by Chevrolet chief engineer Ed Cole, there had been some shortages of specified parts, and the hubcaps were the most obvious. According to Tony Clabber, who drove the first car off the line for the official photographs, the first 25 or so cars produced had these domed caps fitted, and they were also on some of the cars in early publicity pictures.

The second type of wheel cover looked like the final design at a glance, but the Chevrolet emblem was in line with the fake knock-off ears rather than at right angles to them. Fewer than 25 car sets of these covers are believed to have been made, so they are extremely rare. The third type of wheel cover looked like the Motorama car's, with the emblem at 90 degrees to the ears. At some point, possibly late in '54, the chromium-plated eared section started to be manufactured in die-cast zinc, instead of brass.

The early 1950s were the era of whitewall tires and they were a standard fitment to the Corvette for '53. At first US Royal 6.70 × 15 Air Rides with 3in whitewalls were fitted, and later in '53 Firestones too. The whitewall tire became a $26.90 option in '54, but it is not certain that blackwalls were factory-fitted until '55. BF Goodrich also became a supplier during '54 and in the same year there was a change to the safer tubeless tires. Tire pressure was 22psi front and rear and the rating was four-ply.

Tires then had a shorter life than today and were soon replaced. Evidence of original tire fitment is hard to substantiate except with contemporary photographs. Excellent and roadworthy reproductions of the original tires with 3in whitewall bands are fortunately available today.

SUSPENSION & STEERING

The A-arms, uprights and hubs were production items from the passenger car range, specifically the 1949-54 Chevrolets. From 1955 the passenger cars would change to ball joints and rubber bushes, but the two-seater continued with the king pins and threaded bushes until the end of the model in 1962.

Both the upper and lower A-arms were steel stampings and incorporated threaded steel bushes for the cross-shafts. The upper arm was bushed to the top of the spring carrier/cross-member assembly, the lower to a bolted-on cross-shaft. At the outer ends of the A-arms, threaded bushes located the steering knuckle support which housed the king pin on which the steering knuckle pivoted. To provide castor and camber adjustment, the upper outer pivot pin was an adjustable eccentric.

While there were benefits of precise control and location in this old-fashioned arrangement, wear was always a problem and regular greasing and adjustment were of paramount importance. The best dehumidified or heated dry storage allows grease to dry up, preventing penetration of fresh grease and causing premature wear. All parts are available for re-bushing and king pin replacement, but the work is tedious.

The front coil springs, rated at 300lbs, had a free length of 13.45in and 9.75 coils. Delco telescopic shock absorbers were located within the springs; the frail bottom mounting brackets retained by a single bolt were always liable to cracking. A front stabilizer bar located behind the radiator, rubber-bushed to the frame and the front of the lower A-arms, helped control body sway.

The rear suspension was by two semi-elliptic four-leaf springs located outboard of the frame rails, measuring 51in long and 2in wide, and rated at 115lbs. The shackle was at the rear in tension, locating the rear of the spring higher than the front. According to Maurice Olley, this was to ensure some understeer, for directional stability. Delco telescopic shock absorbers were mounted inboard at an inclined angle, which might have given a little lateral location, for otherwise there was none. A rear sway bar was not fitted until 1960.

The steering box was a conventional Saginaw unit with a faster 16.0:1 ratio giving 3.9 turns lock to lock. Compare this with a 1993 Corvette, which has 2.0 turns lock to lock, and power steering to make it possible. The track rod was divided, and operated by an idler arm with an impressive and expensive double-row ball bearing, which was in turn driven by a ball-jointed adjustable link from the Pitman arm. For today's drivers the play at the steering wheel rim can be alarming at first, but when everything is in good order it is remarkably precise.

BRAKES

The brakes were taken straight from the 1953-56 passenger cars, using the same 11in diameter drums all round. The single master cylinder had a 1in bore. At the front the slave cylinders had a 1.125in bore and the shoes were 2in wide. There was slightly less meat at the rear, where slave cylinders were 1in and shoes 1.75in. The effective brake lining area was 158sq in and the rear brakes had 47 per cent of the effectiveness of the fronts. The under-dash parking brake lever operated a mechanical linkage on the rear shoes via levers and cables.

The Corvette weighed 570lbs less than the four-door Bel Air, so it can be surmised that the brakes were not inadequate by the standards of the time. However, the fiberglass Chevrolet also had a lower frontal area than the sedan, so its brakes had to work harder to compensate.

OPTIONS

While in later years the option list on the Corvette ran to dozens of items, enabling buyers to personalize their new cars, and the corporation to reap substantial extra profit, for '53 and '54 all options were built into all cars. Though customers might have been attracted by the base price of $2774.00 for the '54, they had to pay an extra $480.10 to own one. Interestingly, this was still a $480.45 saving on the full price of the '53.

Late in '55 some 75 manual transmission V8s were built, netting their customers a $178.35 saving over the optional automatic, and possibly 10 of the six-cylinder cars were assembled for a saving of $135.00. The only true option of this era, therefore, was the '55 availability of 290B whitewall tires – such a symbol of the period – at $26.90.

Options throughout the 1953-62 period were designated Factory Optional Accessories (FOA) or Regular Production Options (RPO), with Limited Production Options (LPO) being added from 1958. Year by year options and prices are listed in the panel below.

OPTIONS

1953

Code	Option	Quantity	Price
2934	Corvette convertible	300	$3498.00
FOA 101A	Heater	300	$91.40
FOA 102A	Radio, signal-seeking	300	$145.15

1954

Code	Option	Quantity	Price
2934	Corvette convertible	3640	$3498.00
FOA 100	Direction signals	3640	$16.75
FOA 101A	Heater	3640	$91.40
FOA 102A	Radio, signal-seeking	3640	$145.15
RPO 290B	6.70x15 whitewall tires	3640	$26.90
RPO 313M	Powerglide automatic	3640	$178.35
RPO 420A	Parking brake alarm	3640	$5.65
RPO 421A	Courtesy lamps	3640	$4.05
RPO 420A	Windshield washer	3640	$11.85

1955

Code	Option	Quantity	Price
2934-6	Corvette convertible (six)	–	$2774.00
2934-8	Corvette convertible (V8)	–	$2909.00
FOA 100	Direction signals	700	$16.75
FOA 101	Heater	700	$91.40
FOA 102	Radio, signal-seeking	700	$145.15
RPO 290B	6.70x15 whitewall tires	700	$26.90
RPO 313	Powerglide automatic	700	$178.35
RPO 420A	Parking brake alarm	700	$5.65
RPO 421A	Courtesy lamps	700	$4.05
RPO 420A	Windshield washer	700	$11.85

1956-1957

By the middle of the decade the Corvette was looking a little slab-sided and plain. The curves of the body were somewhat soft and ill-defined, and the body shape did not take full advantage of the potential of fiberglass construction. The car had been unchanged for three model years at a time when all models from every American manufacturer were restyled annually.

A styling revolution was sweeping through the industry, with the big three competing on the appearance of their products as much as on performance. Talented designers were hired direct from art colleges and given the chance to see their ideas become reality. The 1955 Chevrolet achieved its classic status because it was so carefully designed. Previous models had been refinements of pre-war shapes, but the '55 was a bold and fresh design for a brave and prosperous new world. Curves had become crisper and shapes were better defined, with chromium strips now used for highlighting.

The 1956 Corvette had to be something very special indeed, particularly as the Corvette was now Chevrolet's most expensive car as well as its image-builder and styling flagship. Apparently the facelift was

done very quickly, once the decision had been taken to continue Corvette production and launch a '56 model. Working on the tenth floor of the GM building on Grand Boulevard in downtown Detroit, the stylists achieved a complete restyle of the car that instantly made it appeal to a more enthusiastic and critical breed of buyer, and established the tradition that would make the Corvette the best-selling sports car of the 20th Century.

There is no doubt that Ford's Thunderbird spurred Chevrolet to fight back with a radically improved Corvette. First seen at the Detroit Auto Show in February 1954, the T-Bird was in production by September 1954. Design work is said to have started on it within a month of the Corvette's 1953 public début at the Motorama in New York, and Ford, with an overhead-valve V8 available and one of the most romantic names ever attached to a car, must have known that it had a potential winner. Indeed, the T-Bird sold over 16,000 units in the 1955 model year compared with a total of only 4640 Corvettes produced in three years by Chevrolet. It was a better looking car and even today much nicer to drive. Fortunately, Ford would go on to mess it up in 1958,

Skilful styling – updating and refining without changing too much – transformed the external surfaces for 1956. Details such as wheel openings now reflected commitment to fiberglass body construction.

Side view shows well that cove was a bold but successful idea; windshield was less raked than previously, and Two-Tone Paint Combination cost $19.40 extra. At the rear, the '56 had less bumper protection than the previous model, and used the fender over-rider as an exhaust exit. This car is Venetian Red, the most popular color in 1956 – the only year of straight-axle production in which red sold best.

making the T-Bird 1000lbs heavier and giving it four seats, leaving the Corvette unchallenged as America's only mass-produced two-seater sports car for the next four decades.

The T-Bird had decent roll-up windows with electric operation, a powered soft-top, a detachable hard-top and a bench seat which could seat three if required. The Ford also offered the driver the choice of automatic, manual or manual with overdrive transmission, and located the shift lever on the steering column to make that bench seat usable.

In redefining the Corvette for 1956, the stylists took from this list only what was appropriate for a true sports car in the European sense, avoiding the bench seat and emphasizing instead the separate two-seat arrangement and keeping the shifter on the floor.

Like the 1963 Split-Window Sting Ray, the '57 Corvette has become the stuff of legends. No matter that many really knowledgeable car enthusiasts

presented with a '56 and '57 side by side would be unable to tell which was which – the '57 is the one to have!

Blame writers such as myself for this anomalous situation. A thousand hacks have studied the option lists and then written in countless magazines that '57 was the watershed year, the holy grail of Corvetteing, because 10 per cent of cars produced were four-speeds and 16 per cent had fuel injection! Today, most of these writers have never even driven a '57, let alone owned one, so do not despair of your '56 yet!

BODY & TRIM

The new body fitted the same chassis frame but every panel was different, achieving a tauter and more eager appearance. The headlights were brought forward and emphasized with their own round chromium-plated rims, and the parking lamps were moved directly

beneath them. On early production '56 cars the headlight rims were painted body color.

The hood was given twin longitudinal bulges in a style strongly reminiscent of the contemporary Mercedes 300SL. Behind the front wheel opening and running back into the door was a sculpted scoop, generally now called a 'cove' and referred to in contemporary advertising as an indent. This was picked out by a stainless steel molding, clipped to the body, which also surrounded the front wheel arch. If Two-Tone Paint Combination RPO 440 was ordered, this cove was painted in silver or beige – depending on body color – for an additional $19.40.

After three years of production when the doors could only be opened by reaching past the side curtains to the internal door release knobs, there were now external chromium-plated handles and door locks conveniently operated by the ignition key. Winding flat glass door windows with the option of power operation replaced the side curtains, making the '55 Corvette the last American production car in more than 50 years to use them. The doors now opened on pop-out hinges to make entry and exit easier; the same principle had been used on the hood since the beginning.

On top of each front fender was the only non-functional styling gimmick on the car – air scoops the same as were seen on the 1953 Motorama show car, but which had not made production on the '53-'55. Accounts from the time suggest that these scoops were intended to be functional air intakes for the interior, but they were probably closed off for reasons of cost and, even more likely, because being in a low-pressure area meant that they simply did not work.

The wheel openings in both the front and rear fenders on the '56 had the plain, crisply cut edges which identified the body as being made of fiberglass and then became a Corvette trademark. As the '53 body had been designed to be fabricated from pressed steel if required, its wheel openings carried the characteristic rolled shape of metal construction. The effect of the plain edge was to emphasize the new Corvette's elegant shape, which was helped by the swept-back rear of each wheel opening.

At the rear, the 'futurist' light pods were removed and the lights were instead neatly dropped into scoops in the reshaped fenders. The rear light pods had previously been individual moldings which were bonded onto the body in a separate operation and the joint then filled before painting; they were out of character for a pure and honest reinforced plastic car.

As the previous model had suffered from exhaust fumes being drawn back into the cabin, the opportunity was taken to relocate the exhaust outlets to the rear of the fender pontoons so that the waste gasses could be carried away more easily, instead of discharging into the still air in the wake at the center of the car. Unfortunately nothing was done to relieve the problem of gasoline fumes entering the car when cornering hard to the right with a full tank, owing to

Original and unrestored Cascade Green '56, in enemy territory? Crossed-flag emblem in cove is incorrect but was often added by enthusiasts.

Until April 1956 all that year's convertible top cars came with hydraulic operation, so all but a few hundred '56s have a power top. It was neither easy to use nor reliable when older, and by 1962 fewer than 3 per cent of buyers wanted it. Detail views show the following: top folded into compartment (upper left); under-dash switch for power top (lower left); firewall-mounted circuit breaker (upper centre); limit switches in top compartment (lower centre); folding top cover safety switch, between seat backs (upper right); interconnected hinges – found on all '53-62s – that prevent top cover and trunk lid being opened at the same time, with left-hand bracket connecting top lid to its ram (lower right).

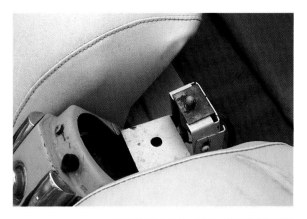

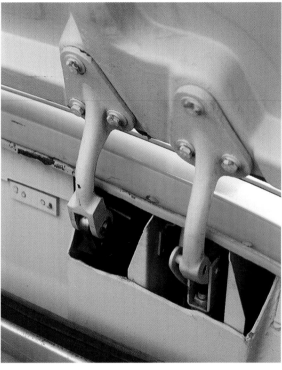

surge in the side-filled, cross-mounted tank. In today's safety-conscious environment it also seems surprising that this tank should be mounted actually within the passenger compartment. Both of these design flaws remained with the model until the end of production in 1962.

The rear bumper was now split and incorporated overriders (bumper guards) above the newly positioned exhaust pipe outlets, reaching up the center line of the fenders. Otherwise, the bumpers were no stronger than previously, in contrast with other 1956 domestic cars whose bumpers were so strong that they were used to jack the car for tire changing.

If the car was one of the 2717 fitted with the RPO 102 radio option, then an antenna was fitted to the top of the left rear fender, in place of the molded-in unit fitted into the trunk lid of the previous model. The trunk lid also lost its complicated license plate housing in favor of a plain bracket to locate it between the split rear bumper.

The shape of the folding convertible top changed with the introduction of two additional bows, which not only improved appearance and reduced overall height, but also made the top easier to erect. However, it still restricted side vision for tall drivers and left a large blind spot between the side and back windows. There was a color choice of black, beige or white for the vinyl-coated material of the top.

Power operation of the convertible top was listed as an option, but at least the first 2500 cars built for the '56 model year had it fitted as standard, manual operation not becoming available again until the end of May of that year, when the hydraulic top became RPO 473. More than 77 per cent of '56s were fitted with the hydraulic convertible top, making this by far the most popular year for this option; by 1962 the proportion had shrunk to a mere 2.4 per cent.

The power system used a trunk-mounted hydraulic pump (powered by a 12-volt electric motor), two solenoid valves, one hydraulic cylinder to control the convertible top cover, two cylinders to power the top itself, two convertible top cover limit

Onyx Black '57 with Inca Silver coves: black was the biggest-selling color in that year, and most cars were sold with optional whitewall tires. Convertible top now had four intermediate bows, making it smoother in appearance as well as easier to erect. Beige, black or white vinyl was the color choice. Revised shape brought numerous practical improvements, such as wind-up windows, handles and door locks. With Onyx Black, interior color choice was beige or red.

switches, two limit switches for the top itself and two safety switches to prevent operation with either the trunk open or the top cover latched shut. The main cylinders were mounted parallel to the seat backs, in compartments behind the doors.

The effect and novelty of the system in use is still dramatic. Before using the dash-mounted switch, the driver is still required to unlatch the top cover and release the two upholstery tabs. He must also hold the rear bow of the top forward after the top is raised to allow the return of the top lid, and at the end of the sequence to latch the front bow and perhaps struggle to reach back and fasten the rear of the top. Not much more work was required to lift the top manually, so it is not surprising that in many cases rams were released from the frame as soon as the system gave trouble. Without the power option the top is still very easy to erect, and can be stowed with practice without the driver leaving his seat.

The blind spot with the convertible top was not a problem for those who ordered the detachable fiberglass hard-top, as it featured a beautifully designed quarter window behind the door window for all-round vision. Mounted at the front with three latches

similar to the convertible top, it was screwed at the rear to the deck lid in three positions and was longer than the soft-top. Like all Corvette hard-tops since, this was a careful and masterful piece of automotive design, subtly changing the appearance of the convertible to which it was fitted. A particularly appealing feature of the hard-top is that, when properly installed, it can be swung into a vertical position by releasing the three latches. This is useful for loading things behind the seats, or just impressing onlookers. The top must be securely propped and this operation should not be attempted in windy weather.

The hard-top was offered either as a $215.20 addition or as a no-cost alternative to the soft-top. If fitting a soft-top to a car that came only with a hard-top, it is necessary to obtain pairs of folding top reinforcements and brackets to mount the hinge arms of the top onto the bodywork on either side of the seat.

Externally on a basic optioned car there were no changes for the '57 model – the car was a true carry-over from 1956. However, if the optional hard-top was fitted, then an immediate difference was apparent at the front of it where there was now a 2in wide stainless steel header trim in place of the anodized and

Early '56s had painted rather than chromium-plated headlamp bezels; original 'T-3' headlamps, once sought-after, are now available in reproduction. New features at the rear were sunken lamps, exhaust outlet through bumper, and conventional (not fully retractable) radio antenna; extra fittings on this deck lid are for mounting a hard-top.

Circular emblem at front and rear was plastic and retained by a three-pronged, chromium-plated metal bezel. Fuel-injected cars proudly proclaimed their power plant with both script and crossed flags on the coves.

COLORS

1956

Body	Cove option	Wheels	Soft-top	Interior	Steering wheel	Dash top	Dash lower
Onyx Black	Silver	Black	Black or White	Red	Red	Black	Red
Aztec Copper	Beige	Copper	Beige or White	Beige	Beige	Copper	Beige
Cascade Green	Beige	Green	Beige or White	Beige	Beige	Green	Beige
Arctic Blue	Silver	Blue	Beige or White	Red	Beige	Blue	Beige
				Beige	Red	Blue	Beige
Venetian Red	Beige	Red	Beige or White	Red	Red	Red	Beige
Polo White	Silver	Red	Black or White	Red	Red	Red	White

1957

Body	Cove option	Wheels	Soft-top	Interior	Steering wheel	Dash top	Dash lower
Onyx Black	Silver	Black	Black or White	Red	Red	Black	Red
			Beige	Beige	Beige	Black	Beige
Aztec Copper	Beige	Copper	Beige or White	Beige	Beige	Copper	Beige
Cascade Green	Beige	Green	Black, White or Beige	Beige	Beige	Green	Beige
Arctic Blue	Silver	Blue	Black or White	Red	Beige	Blue	Beige
			Beige	Beige	Red	Blue	Beige
Venetian Red	Beige	Red	Black or White	Red	Red	Red	Beige
			Beige	Beige	Red	Red	Beige
Polo White	Silver	Red	Black or White	Red	Red	Red	White
		Silver	Beige	Beige	Beige	White	Beige
Inca Silver	Ivory	Silver	Black or White	Red	Red	Silver	Beige
			Beige	Beige	Beige	Silver	Beige

sometimes painted trim on the '56 hard-top. A new color, Inca Silver, was added to the previous six choices, and if code 440 dual color was selected, then the cove was finished in Ivory.

Only a 1957 fuelie could carry 'Fuel Injection' scripts (3742212), and the onlooker was left in no doubt that the car was so equipped. The three scripts were placed on the trunk lid and in both coves, where they were combined with crossed flags (3742213). Sometimes one sees the script mounted above the grille on the front of the car, but this is incorrect. Unfortunately, a diagram showing this location appeared in contemporary parts books for a while.

Parts books and shop manuals, incidentally, are generally a poor guide to originality, because both had to be prepared well in advance of the launch date of the car, prior to small changes often made to the final design. Photographs exist of pre-production prototypes of the '57 with the front-mounted 'Fuel Injection' emblem, but it is certain that none of the 1040 cars sold had this. All carried it more fittingly on the rear.

CHASSIS

The frame was a carryover from the 1955 model, requiring no changes.

CHASSIS NUMBERS	
1956	E56S001001 – E56S004467
1957	E57S100001 – E57S106339

INTERIOR

For 1956, a new waffle-pattern material was introduced into the central portion of the seat cushions, and repeated on the door panels and hard-top headlining. For the first time, the passenger seat as well as the driver's seat were adjustable fore and aft, both seats having the extended top to the seat back to preserve the integrity of the sculpted design of the bodywork behind the seats. The seats were narrower than previously because of the wider doors.

The seat divider now contained a neat lockable glove box, which was added because the doors could no longer accommodate their previous lidded lockers, this space now being required for the window lift mechanism and the lowered window glass. The inner door panels were fixed by self-tapping screws into holes drilled in the fiberglass doors, and soon worked themselves loose. Every restorer has a favorite solution to this problem, and among the best is to bond in captive aluminum threaded plugs.

Powered windows became an option (RPO 426) in 1956, but in fact early cars all had them as they were sent out fully loaded. Between 1957-62, a period through which the powered windows remained unchanged, they were taken up by only 5-6 per cent of buyers. At $59.20 they were not cheap and, like any 40-year-old electrical device, are today prone to trouble, unless completely and properly restored. Those who do not have power windows need not regret it.

Mounted centrally in the dash was the optional signal-seeking AM radio (FOA 102) which now featured transistors – the Corvette was the first GM car to use this new technology. A special plate was mounted over this area if this radio, unique to the year in detail, was not required, but 78 per cent of '56s were fitted with it.

INSTRUMENTS & CONTROLS

The dashboard was very similar to the '55, retaining the same gauges and control knobs with brushed aluminum rather than plastic/chromium centers. But the striking difference for the driver was the sprung steering wheel of more sporting character, with three perforated spokes and rim color matched to the interior. This replaced the steering wheel derived from passenger car use, with its distinctly unsporting chromium horn ring.

On the transmission tunnel there was now a shifter console with integral ash receiver for smokers. The shift knob on both the standard three-speed transmission and the RPO 313 automatic were chromium-plated for 1956 only.

RPO 579E was an option designed for the serious racer only. For road use the most important instrument is the speedometer, which on the Corvette has

Interior of a '56, clearly showing waffle-pattern vinyl seats, also used in '57. A useful lockable map compartment was now incorporated between the seat backs. Wind-up windows, optionally electric, meant the end of door pockets. Door was opened by pulling back the white plastic knob, a Corvette feature until 1968. Swing-out hinges improved passenger access. Interior rear-view mirror had thumbscrew adjustment in '56 (above left), threaded base and lock-nut in '57 (above right). Matching dash pods (below): the 140mph speedometer, here with optional parking brake warning light below, has a needle that does not describe a true arc; grille in front of passenger conceals radio loudspeaker. Dash panel (facing page) was similar to the '53-55 version, but sporty three-spoke steering wheel was strikingly different. Examples shown are from the two model years covered in this chapter: the '56 (upper) has beige lower instrument panel that was part of the red interior package, while the '57 (lower) shows the red finish used only when a red interior was specified on an Onyx Black car.

always been placed directly in front of the driver, with the tachometer at this stage in the car's life still stuck out in the middle of the dash above the radio and between the minor gauges, as it had been in the original Motorama show car, where the principal dash design objective appeared to have been symmetry. But racers need obey no legal speed limits and on the track the tachometer is the instrument that matters. In 1957 the 43 cars built with this option had a large AC rev counter (without total meter) mounted on a special bracket clamped to the steering column. The resulting hole in the dash was covered either by a ¼in thick plastic disc or a circular Corvette trunk emblem.

ENGINES

Perhaps with a view to achieving the maximum impact with its vastly improved new model, at least the first 1650 '56s made were fitted with a dual-carburetor 225bhp version of the 265cu in small-block Chevrolet V8. Only in June 1956 did this engine become an option (designated RPO 469) with the introduction as standard equipment of a new single-carburetor base engine rated at 210bhp. Because the high-performance engine started out as the only one available, I will discuss this first.

By holding back the base engine, for whatever reason, Chevrolet gave the Corvette a boost in any discussion, description or demonstration, and the dual Carter carburetors left no doubt about the direction in which the Corvette was heading. There was further proof of the Corvette's extra muscle when Duntov himself drove a modified version to a two-way average of 150.583mph on the sand at Daytona Beach during the NASCAR Speed Week in February 1956. In March four factory-prepared cars were sent to Sebring to contest the 12-hour endurance race: two finished, and Chevrolet's Campbell-Ewald advertising agency produced its famous 'The Real McCoy' advertisement, featuring a race-stained, grille-less car being frantically serviced in the pits.

The 225bhp engine had a compression ratio of 9.25:1 and an aluminum intake manifold (cast number 3731394) with twin four-barrel Carter carburetors of types 2419S (front) and 2362S (rear, with cold-start choke). Air cleaners were of 6in diameter with four rows of louvers, their cases made of polished aluminum. They were of sealed construction: in other words they were discarded when too dirty to use again.

Starting a 25-year tradition that would identify optional high-performance small-blocks through 1980, this engine had cast aluminum valve covers. These featured a cast-in 'Corvette' script, nine ribs and offset mounting screw holes. Being stiffer than the stock stamped steel covers, the cast units provided much improved oil retention and enhanced the appearance of the engine, giving it a look unique to the Corvette. To prevent interference with the dual-

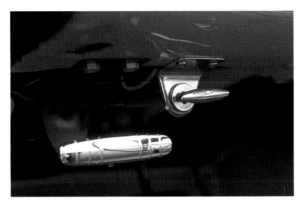

Parking brake and hood release levers on a '57.

carburetor aluminum intake manifold, the upper gasket flange of this valve cover was cut away at about the time this engine became an option.

The cylinder block cast number on all '56s was 3720991; this same block was also used in 1956 Chevrolet cars and trucks. This was the first block to feature a cast-in boss for an oil filter, which was located at the now familiar lower left-hand rear of the engine. The first-phase 225bhp cars had a unique position for the oil dipstick at the right-hand front of the engine, but on later motors this reverted to the more logical place on the driver's side. Why logical? Because after pulling the hood release it is easier to check the oil without having to walk round to the other side of the car, then having to come back to push the hood release handle back in and close the hood. Incredibly, the dipstick reverted to the passenger's side on the 1980 Corvette and has remained there inconveniently on all models since!

Cylinder heads were cast number 3725306 and were also used on the later base 210bhp motor. When the 225bhp motor became option 469 later in the year, it used cast number 3731762 heads. Both of these heads were also used on the full-size 1956 Chevrolet passenger cars. Valve diameters were 1.72in (intake) and 1.50in (exhaust).

The 1956 model year saw the introduction of the classic ram's horn exhaust manifold, a surprisingly free-flowing and symmetrical design made of cast iron. It was destined for a 25-year production history with only minor modifications, but a plethora of cast numbers. The early 240bhp motor (see below) used manifolds (both of cast number 3725563) with two exhaust pipe flange studs, while the later base and optional motors used manifolds (3731557 left, 3731558 right) with three studs. While it is generally true, as explained on pages 31-32, that throughout production GM's part numbering system used odd numbers for left-hand parts and even numbers for right-hand parts, there were exceptions to this rule on any year of Corvette, but these amount only to single figures and are confined to instances where parts from other GM cars, such as window lift motors on '57s to '62s, were adapted and used backward.

As explained above, the base equipment 210bhp motor was not introduced until early in June 1956,

Tachometer drive was normally from the generator (as here), but from the distributor on fuel-injected cars with optional cold air intake box. Windshield washers were an option.

The 225bhp 265cu in small-block with dual four-barrels on an aluminum intake manifold was initially the only option for '56 and all but a few hundred cars were fitted with this motor that year. Ribbed aluminum valve covers had offset mounting holes, and were more oil-tight than the stamped steel type used on base engines. This was also the first year for ram's horn exhaust manifolds. On '56s there was an outside air supply to the optional heater, the hose of which is fitted against the right-hand inner fender.

and it is believed that only 387 were built before the end of the model year. These engines are desirable for reasons other than their rarity. They are nicer to drive on today's roads, something that is true of virtually all of the base equipment carburetor Corvette motors from this one until the last L48 built in 1980. Lower compression ratio, smaller valves, hydraulic valve lifters, softer cam and single carburetor mean easy starting, a sewing machine idle, instant torque in any gear, cooler running in modern traffic and even – if it matters to you as it does to me – better economy and lower emissions.

The 210bhp unit used a single Carter 2366SA carburetor on a cast iron manifold with cast number 3735448. The air cleaner was the same 11in unit as on the 1955 V8. Valve covers were stamped steel with a white outlined 'Chevrolet' script, as used on the passenger cars. Compression ratio was the same 9.25:1 as the 225bhp engine. The cylinder heads were the same small-port design, cast 3725306, as used on the earlier 225bhp engine.

Also listed for 1956 was an optional 240bhp engine, ordered by paying $172.20 for the 225bhp engine (RPO 469) and then adding a further $188.30 for Duntov's new long-duration camshaft (RPO 449). This camshaft was described by Duntov as having been designed several weeks before the Daytona Speed Week, and it was claimed that more

than 100 Corvettes and full-size Chevrolets with it had been delivered to dealers by 1st February to comply with NASCAR's homologation rules. Described by Chevrolet as being for racing purposes only, this camshaft was eventually built into 111 '56 Corvettes. Peak power occurred at 5800rpm and, to quote Roger Huntington in *Sports Cars Illustrated* of July 1956, '…don't try to balance a coin on the hood when it's idling!'

For 1957 the swept volume was increased to 283cu in, achieved by boring the block to 3⅞in instead of 3¾in while retaining the 3in stroke. Cast number for all 1957 blocks was 3731548. The base '57 motor was rated at 220bhp and was a carryover of the previous 210bhp unit, the increased power derived from the larger bore. Only this engine carried the steel valve covers with stamped Chevrolet script. This was the most popular choice with 48 per cent of customers choosing it. Similarly, the 245bhp motor was an enlarged version of the 225bhp dual-carburetor unit of 1956, and now carried the RPO number 469A.

A milestone in Corvette history occurred in 1957 – this was the year of fuel injection. This not only made the engine more powerful, but banished one of the banes of the Corvette racers – fuel surge in the carburetor float chamber. This has long been a problem when a car with a four-barrel carburetor is driven hard round a bend, and centrifugal force of up

For '57 engine size increased to 283cu in: this is the base 220bhp version with single Carter WCFB carburetor, cast iron intake manifold and steel valve covers. Base engines are usually the smoothest, and have the low-end torque to make driving a joy on any roads. Note the kick-down rod that identifies this example as a Powerglide automatic.

ENGINE IDENTIFICATION

Engine block cast numbers

1956	265cu in (V8)	3720991
1957	283cu in (V8)	3731548

Stamped engine number suffixes

1956	265cu in (V8)	FK	210bhp 1x4B carb auto
	265cu in (V8)	GV	210bhp 1x4B carb three-speed
	265cu in (V8)	FG	225bhp 2x4B carb auto
	265cu in (V8)	GR	225bhp 2x4B carb three-speed
	265cu in (V8)	GU	240bhp RPO 469 high-lift cam three-speed
1957	283cu in (V8)	EF	220bhp 1x4B carb manual
	283cu in (V8)	FH	220bhp 1x4B carb auto
	283cu in (V8)	EH	245bhp 2x4B carb manual
	283cu in (V8)	FG	245bhp 2x4B carb auto
	283cu in (V8)	EM	250bhp injection manual
	283cu in (V8)	FK	250bhp injection auto
	283cu in (V8)	EG	270bhp 2x4B carb manual
	283cu in (V8)	EL	283bhp injection high-lift cam manual
	283cu in (V8)	EN	283bhp injection air intake manual

to 1g pushes fuel to the wall of the float chamber. Fuel injection solved this problem at a stroke, and at the same time improved power and responsiveness.

Mercedes-Benz had pioneered fuel injection for road cars in the exotic and expensive 300SL of 1954. The great achievement of American industry in the 20th Century has been to place the luxuries of the rich into the lives of everyman, and offering injection

on the Corvette and other Chevrolets was one more example of this trend. For nine years it was the ultimate option on the affordable sports car and colored the brand image for much longer.

The hydraulic cam version of the fuel-injected 283 – the RPO 579A rated at 250bhp – was the next most powerful engine in the '57 range after the two carburetor units already described. It shared its camshaft and 9.5:1 compression ratio with these engines. When harnessed to the Powerglide automatic, it became RPO 579C.

The final two optional motors both used the Duntov camshaft – known as the optional competition cam – with solid valve lifters. The dual-carburetor version was the 270bhp RPO 469C, which sold 1621 units, and the injected version was the 283bhp RPO 579B. This latter engine achieved its impressive output by the use of a high-compression head (cast number 3731539) which raised the ratio to 10.5:1. The output of this motor, in fact, is believed to have been more like 290bhp, but 283 was the figure chosen: interestingly, no other Corvette power output has ever been advertised to single-digit accuracy (the quoted figure is normally rounded to the nearest '5'), and indeed engine dynamometers are still not sufficiently accurate to justify such precision, particularly if one is averaging a number of full-power passes on the machine.

A final engine-related option number was 579E. As well as the special tachometer described earlier, this $726.30 package included a cold air intake box – the coveted 'air box' – which fed a denser charge of cold outside air from in front of the radiator into the injection air meter. Cars fitted with this package were intended for racing and did not have radios, or, therefore, ignition shielding. Almost uniquely among small-block engines fitted to Corvettes, the plug wires on these cars passed over the valve covers, not underneath the exhaust manifolds.

ELECTRICS

Distributors on all motors but the later 210bhp unit had dual ignition points for a better high-speed spark. The distributor and ignition wires and plugs were protected from interfering with radio reception by ignition shielding. This was fitted as standard on approximately the first 1650 cars with the early 240bhp motor, but then became part of the FOA 102 optional radio package. After the beginning of June 1956, no Corvette had shielding unless it was fitted with a radio – but this was the majority of cars.

The three-section telescopic radio antenna was mounted in the top of the left rear fender. Cars fitted with radios also had static collectors in the front wheel hubs.

TRANSMISSION

The manual three-speed Saginaw gearbox, the same unit fitted to the few late '55 stick shifts, was the base no-cost transmission for 1956. A new shift console incorporated an ashtray with a hinged lid. Apart from the first few cars produced which used the 1955 white plastic knob, it is generally agreed that the '56 shift knob was chromium-plated zinc.

The Saginaw three-speed is a surprisingly pleasing gearbox to use and suits the wide torque band of the base 230bhp single-carburetor motor. It always has a nice shift, and the position of reverse and non-synchromesh first – opposite each other on the left side of the 'H' – makes it the perfect 'box for low-speed maneuvering. The Saginaw was made in a specific Corvette version with the main case (cast 3743368) containing close-ratio gears with a 2.21:1 first gear, and a tail housing (cast 3737450) with bosses to mount the shifter. No other Chevrolet at that time used a floor shift, all others being mounted on the steering column. This transmission continued unchanged through 1960.

Much is made of the mistake that Chevrolet made in not offering a manual shift option for the 1953 and '54 models, so it is interesting to note that approximately half of all '56 Corvettes were still ordered and sold with the Cleveland-built Powerglide two-speed

Fuel injection for '57 was a technological tour de force for General Motors, setting new standards for power (283bhp) and economy. One of just 1040 built that year, this is a radio delete car so it has no ignition shielding, and the later type of air cleaner with open element is fitted.

Shifters for Saginaw three-speed manual (right) and Powerglide two-speed automatic (below right) transmissions. Shift knobs in chromium-plated zinc are often seen in straight-axle Corvettes, but are correct, regardless of transmission type, only in '56s built from early February (as shown) and in approximately the first 200 '57s; the '57 automatic illustrated has the correct white Tenite plastic knob. This has been a much discussed topic over the years…

automatic. Maybe it was acceptable to drive an automatic version once the car was empowered with the strong sporting image of the stick shift, particularly as it was hard to tell the difference from the outside.

The Powerglide was the same unit that was used in later '55 production. The shifter was fixed to the tail housing of the transmission and had a chromium-plated ball. The shift pattern remained R-L-D-N-P, two different shift indicator plates being used during the year. The automatic shifter shared the same console as the manual.

The rear axle unit was similar to the previous year's, with a standard ratio of 3.55:1 (stamped AE) or, as a no cost option (RPO 471), a taller 3.27:1 ratio that provided a theoretical top speed of 127mph at peak power.

The availability of a new four-speed transmission from 10th April 1957 benefited the perceived value of the Corvette as a true sports car, and confirmed it as one that could actually be raced. Although the introduction date for the four-speed was well past the halfway point of the model year and only 10.5 per cent of '57s were fitted with it, in the following year it outsold the three-speed.

Borg Warner built the new four-speed transmission and called it the T-10. Synchronised on all forward gears and designed to give years of trouble-free service, it is one of those classics of post-war American industrial design that have proved themselves through their longevity. It was slowly developed to an aluminum case for the 1960s, then ripped off by GM as the Muncie, then uprated to the Super T-10 for the 1970s, then given an overdrive and used in the 1984-88 Corvette as the Doug Nash Engineering 4+3 – and it is still available today as the Richmond four-speed. Because virtually all the same gaskets fit this 40-year production run and almost no part has seen more than one design change, it almost rivals the Chevy small-block itself for legend status.

In its 1957 form, the T-10 had a cast iron casing identified with 'T-10-1 W.G. DIV'. A month and day cast was incorporated below this on the main case. Plant, month, day, year and shift were also stamped on the upper rear left of the main case. The tail housing was at first cast iron and then aluminum by about June. The shifter had no reverse lock-out, and used a white plastic shift knob, the same as on the other '57 transmission choices.

The four speed T-10 is an easy-to-fit replacement for the Saginaw, and in the 40 years since many have been retro-fitted to original three-speed cars. If a car with a serial number prior to approximately E57S103500 has a four-speed, then it is probably not original. On a later car it may be original, but there is no sure way to prove it. Indeed, if you met the first owner of your '57 and he proudly told you about the day in July of that year when your three-speed had been converted to a four-speed, would you really want to convert it back for the sake of pure factory-fresh originality?

The Powerglide automatic transmission continued unchanged for 1957 apart from the November 1956 switch to a new design of stamped aluminum shift indicator plate. In 1957 some 1393 owners – 22 per cent of total sales that year – opted to spend the extra $188.30 to have the shifting done for them.

WHEELS & TIRES

For 1956 one significant external change was the introduction of new wheel covers with fake knock-off spinners, which would remain in use, with only one change, throughout production of the live axle model. Unlike the earlier full wheel covers, they had a plain retaining ring which engaged with four nibs pressed into the outer wheel rim.

If your '57 was one of only 55 ordered with the optional 5.5in wide wheels (RPO 276), then these were readily identified by their Plain Jane small hubcaps. In case use of the word 'small' misleads, it should be pointed out that this is one of the rarest and most desirable of any Corvette options – in the bigger and faster world of performance cars very few sought-after versions are described by the diminutive!

Part numbered 3748348, these optional wheels had an offset of 0.44in instead of the 0.56in of the stock 5in wheel, and their extra ½in width allowed the

Hubcaps on '56-58 cars have no ventilation slots around the perimeter.

fitting of 7.10 tires. The standard Chevrolet small hubcaps (part number 3731847) were used because these wheels lacked the four nibs on the rim which retained the full wheel covers, but they also lent the wheels a more aggressive air. As well as reducing unsprung weight, the smaller hubcaps were less likely to fall off when the wheels inevitably flexed during very hard cornering.

Both sizes of wheel were manufactured by Kelsey Hayes and were supplied in sets of five. Whereas 5.5in wheels were believed to have been painted black only, the 5.0in stock wheels were normally painted to coordinate with the body color. Polo White cars had red or silver wheels depending on the interior trim color chosen.

Basic equipment tires were blackwall 6.70×15. Whitewall tires were optional as RPO 294 and the band varied from 2in to 2¾in width. Suppliers were Firestone, US Royal or BF Goodrich.

SUSPENSION & STEERING

For 1956 two important modifications were introduced by the now legendary Zora Arkus-Duntov. He fitted wedges between the frame and the front suspension cross-member assembly to increase steering castor, which had the effect of improving the directional stability of the car and increasing the self-centering of the steering. He also used his experience to engineer the modification of the front eye mounting of the rear spring, raising it higher to further improve handling.

For the racer there was the option of Heavy Duty Brakes and Suspension (RPO 684), covered in the next section.

BRAKES

The standard braking system was unchanged for 1956 and '57, and performed well in road use. Until the Corvette went to disc brakes in '65, its drums were the same as those on the 500lb heavier full-size Chevrolets, and they are more than adequate in the lighter sports car, even on today's roads.

If you wanted to take your Corvette racing, however, the brakes were rather less effective. There was no problem making the car go fast: with nearly 300bhp available under the driver's right foot, combined with a wide torque band, there was not much around to match a fiberglass '57. But slowing down again was another matter: after the first few corners the drums would expand with the heat, the linings on the shoes would start to cook, and the brake pedal would disappear to the floor.

So it was that the Heavy Duty Brakes and Suspension option (RPO 684) was introduced in March 1957, and it sold a total of 51 units. Earlier in the model year, in November 1956, another option (RPO 581) had been available, but no production figures are available for this. RPO 581 had consisted of stiffer front and rear springs, uprated shock absorbers, a thicker front sway bar and a quick steering adapter which increased the steering ratio to 16.3:1. This option had been fine as far as it went, but had failed to address the most pressing problem for the circuit racer – the brakes. Now RPO 684 delivered a serious attempt to cure this deficiency. Described in contemporary sales literature as 'not recommended for ordinary pleasure driving', it was only available with the 270 dual-carburettor and 283 injection motors, and only with a limited slip differential.

Brake linings front and rear were changed to ceramic/metal composition, distinguished by the lining material being bonded to the shoe in blocks, two on the primary (front) shoe and four on the secondary (rear) shoe. The cast iron brake drums at both front and rear were finned to give a greater surface area to dissipate heat, and the brake backing plates were ventilated, the openings being protected with metal gauze screens.

The dramatic part was the forced air ventilation to the brakes. At the front, rubberized canvas 'elephant ears' with steel reinforcement were provided to deflect cooling air into the backing plates, and similar, though smaller, steel ears were fitted at the rear. An elaborate system of ducts led the cooling air from the front radiator support panel, along the top of the inner fenders, through the rocker panels and into special ducts which deflected the air towards the rear backing plate ears. To modern eyes, it seems that the internal resistance of all these ducts would seriously hinder the effectiveness of the rear brake cooling air, but this does not affect the rarity and desirability of this option.

It may have been galling, though, when Jaguar that same year presented its XK150 with all-round disc

A 1957 Wonder Bar radio: signal seeking was achieved by pressing the bar at the top; the name was a bad pun on the German for 'wonderful'.

brakes, which cooled themselves and needed no special ducting. It would be eight more years before the Corvette would have disc brakes...

OPTIONS

Many options have been discussed through this chapter, but the full list of options available for the 1956 and '57 model years is given in the panel.

OPTIONS

1956 Code	Option	Quantity	Price
–	Corvette convertible	3467	$3120.00
FOA 101	Heater	–	$123.65
FOA 102	AM radio, signal-seeking	2717	$198.90
FOA 107	Parking brake alarm	2685	$5.40
FOA 108	Courtesy lights	2775	$8.65
FOA 109	Windshield washers	2815	$11.85
RPO 290	Whitewall tires	–	$32.30
RPO 313	Powerglide automatic	–	$188.50
RPO 419	Auxiliary hard-top	2076	$215.20
RPO 426	Power windows	547	$64.60
RPO 440	Two-tone paint	1477	$19.40
RPO 449	High-lift cam with 469	111	$188.30
RPO 469	225bhp 2x4B carb motor	3080	$172.20
RPO 470	White or beige soft-top	2735	No cost
RPO 471	3.27:1 axle ratio	–	No cost
RPO 473	Power convertible top	2682	$107.60

1957 Code	Option	Quantity	Price
–	Corvette convertible	6339	$3176.32
FOA 101	Heater	5373	$118.40
FOA 102	Wonder Bar radio	3635	$199.10
FOA 107	Parking brake alarm	1873	$5.40
FOA 108	Courtesy lights	2489	$8.65
FOA 109	Windshield washers	2555	$11.85
RPO 276	15x5.5in wheels	51	$15.10
RPO 290	6.70x15in whitewall tires	5019	$31.60
RPO 313	Powerglide automatic	1393	$188.30
RPO 419	Auxiliary hard-top	4055	$215.20
RPO 426	Power windows	379	$59.20
RPO 440	Two-tone paint	3026	$19.40
RPO 469A	245bhp 2x4B carb motor	2045	$150.65
RPO 469C	270bhp 2x4B carb motor	1621	$182.95
RPO 470	White or beige soft-top	3588	No cost
RPO 473	Power convertible top	1366	$139.90
RPO 579A	250bhp fuel injection manual	182	$484.20
RPO 579B	283bhp fuel injection	713	$484.20
RPO 579C	250bhp fuel injection auto	102	$484.20
RPO 579E	283bhp fuel injection	43	$726.30
RPO 677	3.70:1 Positraction	327	$48.45
RPO 678	4.11:1 Positraction	1772	$48.45
RPO 679	4.46:1 Positraction	–	$48.45
RPO 684	Heavy Duty Brakes & Suspension	51	$780.10
RPO 685	Four-speed T-10 transmission	664	$188.30

1958-1960

By 1958 the US economy was booming, the national mood was one of self-confidence and General Motors was as successful as ever. Its cars were also becoming bigger: the full-size, four-door Chevrolet grew in length by 15in and added 350lbs of weight between 1954-58, and all models were becoming lower and wider. Superb design though it may have been, the Corvette was now Chevrolet's image-builder and had to reflect something of the corporate look.

Like arch rivals Ford, and almost all of the GM range, Chevrolet adopted quad headlamps for 1958 and the Corvette had to have them too. There were howls of anguish from the press who could see no good reason why 'the corrosive influence of the stylists' should be loosed on such a pure form, particularly after a production run of only two years, but clearly Chevrolet thought it knew what America wanted. The need for annual innovation was paramount, particularly as 1958 was GM's golden anniversary year. The '57 was an almost perfect shape, but had it been left untouched it would have soon become old-fashioned and atrophied, and maybe the Corvette would have died. These were times of rapid change, growth and innovation.

The Styling staff were constantly presented with an almost impossible task by the annual model change. If they produced perfection, they would struggle to improve it for the following model year. If they could not improve it, then they had to change it anyway. As the decade passed, the cost of these model changes became apparent into the 1960s and annual updates with major changes every three or four years became the pattern for the big-selling models. The limited-production Corvette was happily allowed to run for years without major change, to the continuing joy of parts specialists...

Twenty years ago the '57 was revered as the ultimate Corvette and everything that followed it was thought to be somehow less than perfect, but tastes have changed. Recently I had a '57 to sell, and 'phoned a list of six people who had all said they wanted a '58 to '60 model. To offer them a '57 for the price of a '58 should surely have seen the car sold quickly, but not one of them would consider it – they had to have the quad headlamps and the big bumpers. I have to admit that I too prefer the later car, though mainly because I love driving behind that superb instrument panel binnacle with its concentric speedo and tacho.

The quad-headlamp '58 Corvette was slightly longer, wider and more flamboyant. The bumpers were at last big enough to protect the body, and were supported by strong brackets.

DIMENSIONS

Length	177.20in
Width	72.8in
Height	51.5in
Wheelbase	102in
Max track	59in
Curb weight (auto)	3135lbs

Grille in cove was not functional, but restored the shape of the wheel arch to protect the cove from road mud. Two-Tone Exterior Paint, giving a contrasting color for the cove, was a $16.15 option selected by a third of new buyers, but most restorers adopt this finish; with no paint code tags on the car as a guide, final color is the owner's choice. Front part of cove was often seen painted body color, but this was never correct. Note lack of sun visors, which were an option until 1961.

BODY & TRIM

The changes for 1958 were considerable and increased the length of the car by 9in, the width by 2¼in inches and added 200lbs to the overall weight.

The front of the car was cleverly restyled to accommodate four 5¾in sealed beam headlamps, which were a real improvement for night driving. The outer lamps contained dipped and main beam filaments, while the inner pair had single filaments and were lit only when main beam was selected with the floor-mounted switch. The lamps were surrounded by chromium-plated, cast zinc-alloy bezels which were slotted to receive the front of the tapered stainless steel strips that ran back along the fender top almost to the base of the windshield. To make these tapered strips appear straight and true is one of the tests of a first-class restoration.

Below the quad lights were new dummy grilles – or real ones if the Heavy Duty Brakes & Suspension option (RPO 684) was ordered. At a glance the main grille appears to be similar to the previous year's, but it is narrower and has only nine teeth instead of 13. The teeth themselves are the same, with four of the previous year's five separately part numbered teeth

utilized in quantities varying from one to four; starting from the center, there was one of 3706424, two of 3706425, four of 3706427 and two of 3706428. The grille surround was new, being cast in two pieces to accommodate the bumper returns, and the grille center bar was shorter.

New emblems at front and rear were given visual depth by making them up from four separate pieces – bezel, seal, clear emblem and lower dished reflector. The body and trunk lid had holes cut in to accept the emblems and the same bezel (3740239) was used at either end.

The only non-functional adornments on the 1956-57 Corvette, the air scoops on top of the front fenders, were removed for the '58 model. But in their place came a whole lot of new non-functional icons. Most obvious were the vents behind the front wheels, trimmed with three chromed spears on either side. They effectively filled in part of the side cove, restoring the true shape to the rear of the front wheel opening when compared with the '57, but they served no air outlet function – air coming into the engine compartment through the grille was more than adequately evacuated through the open underside of the engine compartment.

Roman Red with White cove and whitewall tires makes a superbly balanced composition in side elevation. Externally '59 and '60 models are identical except for wheels: black on '59s, body color (as here) on '60s. Fuel injection emblem on the front fender identifies the power within, and perfect curves of the tail make the '59-60 model the most desirable to many.

Matching red speedo nacelle and steering wheel catch the eye in the front view of this Tuxedo Black Two-Tone '60. On a sunny day on a tree-lined back road, reflections interact between this nacelle and the windshield – a visual thrill never experienced by those who trailer their '58-62s. The '60 model was a landmark in the Corvette's slow climb towards popularity: sales that year exceeded 10,000 units – the original target for 1954 – for the first time. The Corvette was now a well-developed sports car able to take on the best of the world, and optional fuel injection put it technically ahead of the rest.

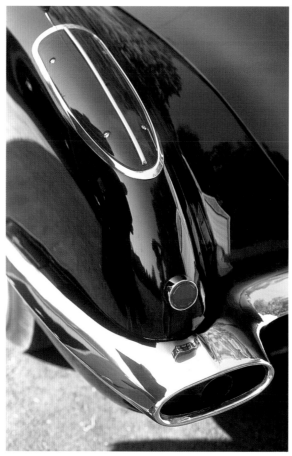

Paired sealed-beam 5¼in headlamps offended contemporary commentators, who felt that the Corvette's clean lines had been spoiled. Exhaust outlet through bumpers may have caused corrosion, but looked great; reflectors were added after the start of '58 production.

Once again the coves were surrounded with stainless steel trims, and when optional Two-Tone exterior paint was ordered the whole area inside the trim was painted silver, ivory or black in 1958, silver or ivory in 1959 or a range of colors in 1960, all to coordinate with the main body color. Over the years it became popular to paint only the recess of the cove in the contrasting color, but this was never how the cars left St Louis. It must be added that no trim identification plate was fitted to any of the cars covered in this book, so no-one can say your car is the wrong color unless there is documentary proof relating to it.

The center rear of the 1958 hood panel received 18 raised louvers, generally known as a 'washboard'. Fortunately these were not functional: the ignition distributor would have been regularly soaked, and engine heat and fumes would have been drawn into the cowl passenger air intake. A significant improvement to the hood was a change to plain hinges: previously, it had been hard to retain good panel fit while adjusting the hood so that the front edge did not catch when it popped out. With a plain front hinge, where the front few inches dropped down when the hood was lifted, adjustment of fit was simplified.

Where the 1956-57 model's bumpers had been skimpy and bolted to the fiberglass, now they were immense and bolted through to the frame. As a consequence, on the production line they had to be fitted after the body was dropped on to the frame rather than before it. The exhaust, which had exited through the vertical bumperette, now came out through an oval aperture in a complex chromed bumper which stretched from license plate to wheel opening on

Two '58-only features that were dropped after a year, but owners love them – washboard effect on hood and twin chromium-plated trunk spears.

either side. As on Cadillacs of the era, steam and acid from the exhaust gases would rust away the rear bumper quickly unless extensions were fitted to the tailpipes. Despite this, the bumper exhaust outlet was a great styling feature, and use of the exhaust pipe as a design element has continued with most Corvettes to the present.

COLORS

1958

Body	Cove option	Wheels	Soft-top	Interior
Charcoal	Silver	Silver	Black or White	Charcoal, Blue-Gray or Red
Snowcrest White	Silver	Silver	Black, White or Blue-Gray	Charcoal, Blue-Gray or Red
Silver Blue	Silver	Silver	White or Blue-Gray	Charcoal or Blue-Gray
Regal Turquoise	White	Silver	Black or White	Charcoal
Panama Yellow	White	Silver	Black or White	Charcoal
Signet Red	Silver or White	Silver	Black or White	Charcoal
Inca Silver	Black	Silver	Black or White	Charcoal, Blue-Gray or Red
Black	Silver	Silver	Black or White	Charcoal, Blue-Gray or Red

1959

Body	Cove option	Wheels	Soft-top	Interior
Tuxedo Black	Silver	Black	Black or White	Black, Blue or Red
Classic Cream	White	Black	Black or White	Black
Frost Blue	White	Black	White or Light Blue	Blue or Red
Crown Sapphire	White	Black	White or Turquoise	Turquoise
Roman Red	White	Black	Black or White	Black or Red
Snowcrest White	Silver	Black	Black or White	Black, Red, Blue or Turquoise
Inca Silver	White	Black	Black or White	Black or Red

1960

Body	Cove option	Wheels	Soft-top	Interior
Tuxedo Black	Silver	As body	Black, White or Light Blue	Black, Blue, Red or Turquoise
Tasco Turquoise	White	As body	Black, White or Light Blue	Black or Turquoise
Horizon Blue	White	As body	Black, White or Light Blue	Black, Blue or Red
Honduras Maroon	White	As body	Black or White	Black
Roman Red	White	As body	Black or White	Black or Red
Ermine White	Silver	As body	Black, White or Light Blue	Black, Blue, Red or Turquoise
Sateen Silver	White	As body	Black, White or Light Blue	Black, Blue, Red or

Apart from optional fuel injection emblems (this style was used through '58-61), chromed scripts were absent from the Corvette. Effective three-piece badges were used instead at front and rear.

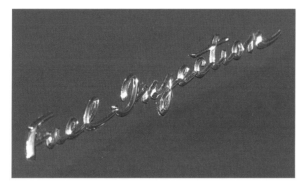

On the trunk lid there were now two chromium-plated longitudinal ribs which ran down to meet the bullet bumper ends at either side of the license plate. While these suggested to the observer that they might be part of an extra luggage rack system, they were not. For 1959 both the washboard on the hood and the chromed trunk ribs were discarded, improving the appearance for all except, of course, those who own '58s today, who will hopefully defend their washboard and ribs.

A welcome improvement at the rear was the new tail light design which now used a red lens flush with the body, one of the neatest jobs ever to come out of Detroit. Inside the lamp a second white lens covered the dual-filament bulb. Mounted beneath these lamps were small red reflectors in chromed bezels. These were required because the very flat angle of the red tail lamp lens did not permit the incorporation of an effective reflector. It must have taken Chevrolet a while to recognize this problem because separate reflectors were not fitted to the first few '58s to leave the St Louis assembly line.

An external mirror was used on the left-hand side of the car only, the original having its adjusting ball central to the mirror head. Chevrolet's later replacement was offset, but good reproductions of the original are available.

The folding top was essentially unchanged from 1957. Now there was the choice of black or white fabric for each car color, except for cars in Silver Blue (blue-gray or white) or Snowcrest White (all three colors). For 1959 the color range for the soft-top was extended with light blue replacing blue-gray and turquoise added, and this choice continued for 1960. It is hard to find suppliers for the blue-gray or turquoise tops at the time of writing. The power-operated folding top (RPO 473) continued to decline in popularity, with just 12 per cent choosing to pay $139.90 for it in '58, decreasing to 6.5 per cent in '59 and 5 per cent in '60.

The auxiliary hard-top (RPO 419) at first looked the same externally as the 1956-57 version, but initially its headlining was in the pebble grain material used for the rest of the '58 interior. The 1959-60 hard-top, however, looked significantly different in the rear lower bow molding, which goes round the back of the top from door to door. Until the end of '58 production this molding was in three pieces with the two joins at either end of the back window, each covered with a 'Y' piece known as an escutcheon. For '59 and '60 there was a two-piece rear molding with a capping to cover the joint in the center back of the hard-top. At the same time the price of the option increased from $215.20 to $236.75, unless the hard-top was supplied as a no-cost alternative to the soft-top. Later tops also had headlinings that matched the interior trim.

As hard-tops are awkward to store, they have a way of becoming lost or forgotten, and often end up on cars to which they never belonged in the first place. The difference between early and late 1956-60 hard-tops is one of those small facts which can still confound the expert!

While visibility out of the hard-top was vastly better than the soft-top, side window height remained unchanged and side vision continued to be restricted for the taller driver. In hot weather the hard-top was almost literally a glasshouse, and the draft from both side windows and the cowl intake would be in demand to defeat the heat gain from sun and the car's drivetrain.

When the soft-top was ordered with the hard-top, the owner had another problem. Invariably, door window adjustment that was right for one top would not suit the other, and this problem worsened as the car aged. There cannot be too many who still drive their straight-axle Corvettes in the traditional hard-top in winter and soft-top in summer mode, but those who do know that they must adjust the windows to suit the hard-top and then adjust the soft-top to suit the windows.

CHASSIS

The chassis frame was substantially the same as for '57, the only significant changes being modifications required to fix the new, heavier bumpers directly to the frame.

As previously, the serial number was stamped onto the top of the left-hand frame rail beneath the door opening, where it could be seen only by removing the body. Also as previously, a stamped metal plate carrying the same serial number was fixed to the hinge pillar of the driver's door with two cross-headed screws. This was clearly bad practice from the point of view of security, so presumably with this in mind a more secure location was required. The Corvette's fiberglass body could not accept a welded-on plate, and the closest piece of static steel was the outer tube of the steering column, under the hood. Despite the fact that the steering column could be removed with a few minutes' work, this was where the serial number plate was to be found from late November 1959. Earlier in the same year, the St Louis plant stamped the last six numerals of the serial number onto the pad at the front of the engine block – thus began 'matching numbers'.

The front suspension and its integral cross-member (derived from the 1951 Chevrolet) continued unchanged and aluminum wedges were still used to improve the steering castor angle, even until 1962. One cannot help but surmise that almost any manufacturer other than GM would have modified either the cross-member or the frame so that the wedges were not required, leading later to confusion about early and late designs. Instead, GM once again kept it simple, to earn the gratitude of enthusiasts and parts people such as myself for generations after. Indeed, as if running this Corvette frame unchanged for 10 years were not enough, GM ran the next one for 20 years!

INTERIOR

The most striking change to the interior was the all-new dash described in the next section. The new

Serial number continued to be retained with cross-headed screws on driver's side door post, but would move to the steering column under the hood from early 1960. This number is also stamped into the frame.

CHASSIS NUMBERS	
1958	J58S100001 – J58S109168
1959	J59S100001 – J59S109670
1960	00867S100001 – 00867S110261

design necessitated a vertical housing for the radio, clock and heater controls, described in the original sales material as the central control panel.

Because both the heater (RPO 101) and AM radio (RPO 102) were options, cover plates were fitted to the central control panel if these were not ordered. The radio cover plate matched the interior color and incorporated a chromium-plated Chevrolet italic script (part number 3711574). The heater control cover plate had threaded studs which passed through the control holes and were secured by nuts. The heater aperture in the right-hand end of the firewall was also covered if there was no heater.

The heater was the most popular option, with only just over 1000 owners in 1958 declining to pay the extra $100 required for this luxury. As in the '57, the heater controls were in a center panel, with controls for fan speed, heater/defroster and air temperature, the latter controlled by a cable-operated and thermo-static water valve. Fresh air to the heater was supplied by a 4in diameter fabric and wire hose which led from a screened opening beside the radiator along the inner fender to the air control door at the front of the heater box. Many original no-heater cars have since been fitted with heaters for convenience. The heater is powerful and effective, encouraging the car to be used as it should, with the top down as often as possible.

On the 88 per cent of '58 Corvettes not fitted with the power top mechanism, there was a cover over the switch hole under the projecting center part of the soft dash pad above the radio.

The defroster outlets in the dash top pad had been chromium-plated through 1957, but they were now painted to match the interior color. At the extreme ends of the dash top pad were protective end blocks that also helped to retain the windlace seals which ran down the inside front edges of the door openings. On 1958 cars these blocks were chromium-plated metal, but on later cars they were hard plastic. The radio loudspeaker grille was fitted from beneath the pad, with no bezel used to finish this until 1960. This new position for the loudspeaker, which previously had faced the passenger, was also an acoustic improve-

Completely revised interior concentrated all instruments in front of the driver, with a new console above the transmission tunnel to house radio, heater controls and clock. Radio loudspeaker was in dash top, to reflect sound off the inside of the windshield. Dark-colored interior for '58 was charcoal (black was not available until the following year), pressed-in seat pleats were longitudinal, and in this model year Corvette became probably the first production car to be fitted with seat belts as standard. Stylish scoop in front of passenger grab bar had white-painted 'Corvette' letters for '58.

ment, the sound being reflected equally towards both occupants by the windshield. Mounted on the dash to the rear of the loudspeaker grille was the rear-view mirror, a two-piece unit joined by a threaded bar terminating in the adjusting ball.

The nervous passenger now had the reassurance of a substantial padded grab rail spanning the right-hand dash recess. Behind this was a stylish brushed aluminum dash insert with the word 'Corvette' spelled out in expanded capitals – GM graphics have always been among the very best. The letters were filled in with white to match those on the horn cap, but they would become black in the following years.

The seats, which for the two previous years had featured a waffle pattern, now had a directional pattern stitched in the centre panels, the vinyl material (also used for the lining of the optional hard-top) being 'pebble-grained'. The seat pleat pattern on the center panel was different for each model year: it ran fore and aft for '58, from side to side for '59, and fore and aft again for '60, but now with the lower panel also wrapping round the front of the seat squab. Leather was still not available, nor was it offered in any of the years covered in this book. A third interior colour, charcoal, became available for the first time for the more conservative minded.

Seat belts were fitted as standard for the first time in '58, and it is believed that the Corvette was the first production car to have them as original equipment. Anchors for seat belts had been factory-installed since '56, but before '58 the belts themselves had to be fitted by the dealer if a customer required them. The first seat belt fabric was colored steel gray, but during March 1958 an additional color, red, was introduced and remained available for the duration of the year. From 1959 a full range of belt colors was introduced.

While the door itself was a carryover from the '57, the door panel was an entirely new design. A swirl of embossed bright metal contrasted with an upper vinyl panel, while a carpeted kick panel introduced a third element into the design. A stout, chromium-plated, vinyl-covered combined door pull and armrest bolted through the panel into the door. Both door panel and armrest were retained by self-tapping screws fixed into the fiberglass of the door, a design oversight which led to the loosening of these components early in a car's life; various combinations of inserts or captive nuts are now used by restorers to solve this problem. Twin safety reflectors warned following traffic of an open door.

The '58 door panels were made of pebble-grained vinyl matching the seats, while the embossing on the metal trim was a pattern of small squares, each painted black in its center. They were a two-piece design for this year only, becoming one piece for '59. The embossed panel and vinyl theme was extended into the foot-wells, giving an impression of spaciousness which was wholly false, because this car was always short of room for the long-legged.

Carpets for the '58 and '59 models were made of a particularly short-pile, low-loop rayon mixture, matching the interior color and with vinyl bound edges. For '60 a speckled carpet known as 'salt and pepper' was introduced. Not normally noticed until the carpet was removed (maybe for transmission service) was an inspection panel in the underbody over the transmission hump; this feature was discontinued in March 1959.

If anyone knows how to profit from selling cars, it has to be General Motors. Surely an interior courtesy lamp, some wire and two door switches should be part of the basic specification of any expensive sports car? GM did not think so and charged $6.50 for FOA 108, netting just short of $100,000 in three years! Just under half of all buyers elected not to pay to enjoy this convenience, which became base equipment in 1961.

Vacuum-operated windshield washers had been available in 1953 and '54 and returned in 1958 (FOA 109), the optional washers having been foot pump-operated in the intervening period. On carburetor cars the vacuum reservoir and the jar incorporating the vacuum motor were on the driver's side, but on fuel-injected cars they were on the passenger's side to avoid the air cleaner assembly and the washer jar had to protected from the exhaust by a heat shield.

Not available previously, sunshades mounted on the windshield header were put on the option list for 1959 (FOA 261) and graduated to becoming base equipment in 1961.

INSTRUMENTS & CONTROLS

If the Corvette had been short of one thing for the previous five years, it was a decent dashboard. Now Chevrolet delivered one of the all-time classics, one that still rates as a triumph for the American ability to make technology stylish. All the disparate elements that had been slung evenly across the previous instrument panel, all the way to the passenger's side, were now tightly grouped in less than the span of the steering wheel, apart from the radio and heater controls (together with the clock) which were appropriately mid-way between the occupants so that the passenger could adjust them too.

The dominant element in this beautifully designed assemblage was the all-important tachometer. This was the only instrument of interest to the racing driver – and racing images were being so successfully exploited in the Corvette's advertising. The tachometers used with lower-powered motors were driven by a long cable from the back of the generator, while those fitted with the high-performance camshaft had a short cable connected to the drive gear at the base of the distributor; internal gearing of the two types differed to suit these alternative drive methods. Cars not fitted with the high-performance cam had an orange sector on the tachometer starting at 5000rpm.

Beginning 1959, a parcel shelf was provided below the passenger's grab rail, and the four-speed shifter gained a reverse lock-out T-handle. Further details of '59 interior: transverse seat pleats with imitation pressed-in stitching; '58-59 style of metal door trims with embossed squares, together with '59-type of door opening knob, which was relocated forward to the metal-trimmed part of the panel; superb black-filled letters on '59-60 passenger-side dash scoop epitomize how GM's Art & Colour section, established by Harley Earl, excelled in typography.

On the higher-revving cars with solid-lifter cam, the sector started at 6000rpm and the figures read to 8000rpm instead of 7000rpm. The total revolution counter, which had been a Corvette feature since 1953, appeared for the last time on '58s with the 5000rpm orange sector.

Flanking the tachometer were gauges for fuel, coolant temperature, ammeter and oil pressure. The lower half of each of these gauges was brush-finish chromium plating carrying wording for the gauge function. While this arrangement would remain until '62, only the '58 had semi-circular upward projections which just covered the center of each gauge. The tips of the '58 and '59 needles had round ends, but from '60 they were pointed. The instrument glasses were convex in '58, but concave for the later years. Neatly arranged beneath the four minor dials were the light, wiper and ignition switches, and also a cigarette lighter.

Behind the tachometer, and concentric with it, was the semi-circular speedometer reading to 160mph. Dots corresponded to the figures on '58 speedos, but later years would have bars. At rest the speedo needle obscured the green telltale of the left turn signal.

The steering wheel was the same as in the previous two years, and the plastic rim color matched the interior trim. For '58 only, however, the crossed flags and lettering on the plated horn cap were picked out in white rather than black paint.

By adopting this impressive and ergonomic dash cluster, Chevrolet once again proved that it was no longer aping the rival sports cars of the time, which all came from Europe, but was now setting the standards itself. Other sports cars were using bought-in proprietary units and arranging them in front of the driver in plain wooden or metal dashboards, but now the Corvette, with production running at almost 10,000 units a year, could justify its own specially designed instrument components, shared with no other car. The domed upper surface of the instrument binnacle distorts the reflection of passing roadside scenery, adding a delightful dimension to the driver's experience and contrasting with the modern obsession for reflection-free and dull dashes.

ENGINES

If none of the four optional power plants was selected, then the standard 230bhp motor for 1958 was 10bhp more powerful than its 1957 equivalent. These motors were identical in specification apart from the Carter WCFB carburetor changing from 2655-S to 2669-S, which had more generous secondary main jets.

Once again it must be emphasized that the base motor is the one that is the 'honey' to drive. It is not only smooth and easy starting, but has a full 300lb ft of torque at only 3000rpm. Of course, it feels good to boast about your dual fours or your solid lifters, but

Interior of '60 Corvette reverted to longitudinal pleats on seats, which were designed with an extended top so that they remained tight to the deck lid even when adjusted forward.

For '60, dash-top loudspeaker grille had painted bezel, door panel received dimpled metal trim, and 'Corvette' lettering in passenger-side dash scoop had colored bars added above and below; perfect fit of dash covering is the mark of a good restoration.

date had two figures (B-3-58). This year dating convention also applied to cylinder heads and other engine castings.

Air for the engine was cleaned by a new design of aluminum air cleaner, with a diameter of 14in. This had three rows of vents around its perimeter and initially was a one-piece design, with the top pan section crimped over the base plate (part number 1553495). In mid-1960 this unit was replaced by a two-piece design with an AC A98 foam element which was removable for cleaning with kerosene. The early one-piece units contained only aluminum wire as a filtration medium, and the whole unit had to be immersed in solution if attempting to clean it.

As mentioned above, the carburetor for the 1958 230bhp unit was the Carter WCFB S-2669, replaced by the 2818-S for '59 and early '60, then the 3059-S for late '60 through '61. The last year for use of the external fuel filter with removable glass bowl was 1958. The intake manifold for the 230bhp unit was made of cast iron (cast number 3746829) and continued to be used for the base motor through '61.

All 1955-62 base motors had stamped steel valve covers with 'Chevrolet' script painted in orange. For 1958-60 the four optional engines each year had ribbed cast aluminum covers with 'Corvette' script. Until about May 1959 the upper pair of mounting holes on the valve covers were more closely spaced than the lower pair. After this date the covers, and cylinder heads, were rationalized so that the spacing was 8¾in top and bottom.

The 1958 base motor carried the cast number 3748770 on both heads, which were also used on the optional engines. Valve diameter was 1.72in (intake) and 1.5in (exhaust). As with the cylinder block, a single numeral for the year in the cast date code identifies the head as correctly originating from Flint, but two numerals mean that it is incorrectly from Tonawanda. Naturally, the Tonawanda head would not affect the running of the car, but correctness is important if a premium price is being sought. After nearly 40 years many heads do have cracks, particularly around the valve seats, and may need replacement.

For 1959 the same 3748770 head was used and additionally another head with cast number 3755550. Both of these heads had the staggered valve cover mounting bolts. The first cylinder head with equal valve cover bolt spacing carried cast number 3767465, and was used for the balance of 1959 production. All of these heads were also used on 1959 optional engines. The only 1960 heads had cast number 3774692 and were used across the board on all engine options.

The above information is not exhaustive and much research has been published on the subject. It should be remembered that on almost all cast iron GM parts the cast number is not the part number, and that the same cast number will appear on similar parts with different part numbers, reflecting changes in the

for pleasure driving of a 40-year-old car on narrow tires this has to be the ideal motor.

Cylinder blocks for 1958 through '59 carried cast numbers of either 3737739 or 3756519, the second number possibly not having been introduced until mid-to-late '58. The latter number was also used for '60 and through to the end of the 283 engine in the Corvette in '61. Both blocks were used in all horsepower combinations and also in Chevrolet passenger cars when the customer specified the 283cu in V8. Compression ratio was 9.5:1 using cast alloy pistons.

Both blocks were cast in the foundries at Flint or Saginaw, Michigan, and were machined and assembled at Flint. They can be distinguished from blocks with the same casting numbers from the foundry at Tonawanda, New York, by their date coding. Taking 3rd February 1958 as an example, Flint blocks had the year element of the date code as a single figure (B-3-8) while the incorrect Tonawanda block of the same

The 230bhp 283cu in motor of '58, with single Carter WCFB carburetor and stamped steel Chevrolet valve covers. Hood now has plain hinges that simplify adjustment, element cannot be removed from air cleaner, and shielding over ignition shows that this is a radio-equipped car.

molding or machining processes. Because it is decades since Chevrolet has supplied any of these original heads through its parts system, and it is very unlikely that a new original head could be found with its part number label attached, it is much easier to consider such parts by their cast numbers instead. It is very much to the credit of Chevrolet that they can still supply heads over the counter of almost identical appearance and construction as the original, and they will bolt on and work almost 40 years later.

Exhaust manifolds were the same cast iron three-stud ram's horn design introduced in 1956 and used with modification right through 1980 on all small-block Corvettes and on some passenger cars. The left manifold (cast number 3749965) was a 'plain' type, while the right manifold (cast number 3750556) incorporated the generator mount and a heat tube for the automatic choke. Both were used on all 1958-61 cars and the base '62, and for some applications into the Sting Ray period. Exhaust manifolds cast at Flint carry no year identification in their casting date.

Many original exhaust manifolds have been discarded over the past two decades in favor of tubular headers in a vain quest for more power. Many more have been damaged by 'crystallization' of the cast iron between the two center mounting holes, a problem that seems to have become more common since the advent of low lead fuel, which may cause a hotter exhaust. Even on a non-original 'driver', the ram's horn exhaust manifold is remarkably efficient and can be relied on for strong bottom-end torque, and, of course, gives out a better sound under the hood, without the characteristic 'ping' of the tubular header.

During the three-year period covered in this chapter there were four optional engines. Dual four-

barrel carburetors or fuel injection could be combined with either the standard hydraulic or the Duntov solid lifter cams to make four quite different power units.

The first of these was RPO 469. By fitting two four-barrel Carter carburetors (2626S front, 2627S rear) to a cast aluminum manifold, peak power was raised to 245bhp at 5000rpm, compared with 230bhp at 4800rpm for the base motor. The torque figure remained the same but was achieved at 3800rpm rather than 3000rpm. An easily adjusted progressive linkage arranged for the rear carburetor to do most of the work, the front unit only opening in the second stage of pedal movement. The rear carburetor also carried the cold-start choke mechanism. These carburetors were also used in '59 and '60.

Using 'Dual Fours' was a simple and effective way of achieving one venturi per cylinder, with the added advantage that the carburetor synchronization necessary with other multiple carburetor systems was not required. Furthermore, the front Carter could be 'switched off', for economy or if the car was to be used by a less experienced driver, by sliding the adjuster collar forward. For maximum throttle response, the linkage at the front carburetor could be relocated in order that both carburetors could operate simultaneously.

The air cleaner was similar to the single-carburetor version but with two extra depressions in its lid for the mounting studs and wing nuts, and, of course, two holes in its base. Like the single-carburetor version, it was of sealed construction with an oiled wire mesh filtration medium. As with the base motor, it was changed to a replaceable element construction in 1959 using the same AC A98 filter element.

The intake manifold was cast aluminum with cast number 3739653. This was the same as the '57 version and was used also on all Corvettes with dual fours through '61. The finish of this manifold should be natural aluminum. The date casting is on the underside of the manifold, the cast number on the top. This manifold carries a 'W' surrounded by a snowflake, identifying it as a product of Winters Industries in Canton, Ohio. This manifold had also been used on the 1957 full-size Bel Air, when the Corvette engine options had been offered for that model year only.

As with all optional engines, valve covers were of cast aluminum and ribbed, with seven ribs and a 'Corvette' script. On early production cars for '58 the script was only $\frac{1}{32}$in high, but later the height of the letters was increased to $\frac{1}{8}$in.

Mechanically the RPO 469 was otherwise unchanged from the base motor. However, it was fitted with a dual-point 1110891 distributor for better spark at high engine speeds. This distributor had no vacuum advance.

The RPO 469C optional engine was essentially the 469 fitted with the Duntov camshaft and solid valve lifters. This improved engine power to 270bhp

at 6000rpm, but maximum torque was down at 285lb ft at 4200rpm. The Duntov cam was a long-duration design and lift was reduced compared with the hydraulic cam used on the 230bhp and 245bhp versions. Carburetors on the 270bhp motor were Carter WCFB 2613S front and 2614S rear.

All 1958-60 Corvettes fitted with solid lifters came from the factory with straight-through mufflers rather than the reverse-flow type used on hydraulic lifter engines. Naturally, because mufflers are usually the first major component to be replaced, it would be highly unlikely today to find a Corvette of this era still fitted with its original mufflers. In 1960 only, an aluminum radiator with an integral top reservoir was fitted to all Corvettes with solid lifter cams. A pressurized cap was used on the radiator; the overflow tank was not pressurized. Aluminum radiators had the advantage of better heat dispersal, something that was becoming increasingly necessary with higher road speeds and also worsening congestion.

From 1957-60 the 270bhp RPO 469C cost $182.95 against $150.65 for the 245bhp RPO 469. Aided by a delay in introducing the 270bhp unit in '58, the cheaper engine outsold the mechanical cam version by more than two to one, but by 1960 the position was reversed and more owners chose the more powerful version.

The 250bhp RPO 579 Fuel Injection was a carry-over of the motor introduced in 1957. Fuel injection was a radical but successful departure from convention for the hitherto conservative Chevrolet; Mercedes-Benz was the only other manufacturer to have used it on mass-produced cars. Because the technology was in its infancy, research and development was continuous and the detailed design of the Rochester units supplied to the production line, and therefore the part numbers, changed a number of times during each year. Since a complete unit these days costs many thousands of dollars, it is important to research carefully in more detailed sources than this one, and to consult one of the Rochester injection restoration specialists before committing to a unit which might later prove incorrect for the application. A tag on the plenum showed the serial number and part number of the injection assembly.

The 1958 RPO 579 engine was a continuation of the '57 version and used the same 7014800 injection unit as late '57 production; the air meter was stamped 7014801 and cast 7014804, and the fuel meter was stamped 7014802 and cast 7014312. This injection unit was then replaced in the 250bhp application by the 7014900, which had a cranking signal valve mounted in the plenum to assist cold starting by providing additional fuel while the starter motor was operating; the air meter was stamped 7014901 and cast 7014922, and the fuel meter was stamped 7014902 and cast 7014899.

For the '59 model the 7014900 injection unit continued in use until replaced by the 7017200. This

unit incorporated a cast-in siphon breaker, a device which prevented an occasional problem of fuel being drawn into a cooling engine and then causing engine damage on restarting. As a matter of good practice, it is worth fitting a siphon breaker to older fuel injection systems as well. The air meter on this unit was stamped 7017201 and cast 7014922, and the fuel meter was stamped 7017202 and cast 7014889.

Also correct for the 1959 250bhp motor was the 7017300R injection unit. This was a 7014800 unit for a '57 Corvette or '58 passenger car that had not been used in production, and was returned to be re-calibrated by Rochester for use on the 250bhp motor. Stamping and cast numbers were the same as for 7017300 (see below). For the 1960 model year, the 7017200 was continued and then replaced by 7017310, with the same stamped and cast numbers.

Because there was no exhaust cross-over passage as in a conventional carburetor engine, there was no need for the thermostatic heat riser valve below the right-hand exhaust manifold. Like all fuel-injected Corvettes of this period, RPO 579 had an exhaust cross-over or balance pipe between the front down-pipes. All injected cars carried the 'Fuel Injection' script (part number 3746457) above the cove on both front fenders. On these models the windshield washer

bottle and associated steel vacuum tank on the inner fender area were moved from the left to the right side, and the plastic bottle protected from the exhaust manifold by an aluminum heat shield.

The ignition distributor was an 1110195 with a single set of contact breaker points and a vacuum advance unit which incorporated the essential drive cable for the injection pump.

By fitting the Duntov camshaft and solid lifters to the RPO 579 fuelie, and raising the compression ratio to 10.5:1, an extra 40bhp was released to make RPO 579D the most powerful engine option. That this motor was of a quite different character to the base engine can be seen from its lowly 290lb ft of torque, not achieved until 4400rpm, and the impressive power peak of 290bhp reached at 6200rpm. The higher compression ratio was achieved by using domed pistons with machined valve reliefs; the cylinder head remained unchanged.

Yet another distributor (part number 1110914) was used with this engine, and had dual points and no vacuum advance. As well as provision for the cable drive to the injection pump, this distributor also had a drive for the tachometer, resulting in a shorter cable and more accurate reading than the generator-driven type used on the other cars.

Fuel-injected motor from '59, the last year that injection could be combined with automatic transmission. Six differently numbered injection units were used for two different horsepowers during the year, such was the pace of development by Rochester.

Right-side view of '59 fuelie shows tachometer drive from distributor, not generator, on injected cars. Injected Corvettes are extremely desirable, with instant torque, more abundant and smoother power, and better fuel economy. Sadly, the injection units were often misunderstood and discarded when only a few years old.

Block and head numeration continued as for the other optional motors but, as with the 250bhp injected motor, there were variations over the three years in the Rochester fuel injection units, due to constant improvement or conversion of one type to another as sales demanded.

In 1958 the RPO 579D injection started as 7014800R, a reworked version of the '57 7014520; the air meter was stamped 7014801 and cast 7014388, and the fuel meter was stamped 7014802 and cast 7014312. Next came the 7014900R, which was a re-calibrated version of the 250bhp 7014900 and used the same numbers for air and fuel meters. The last unit for '58 was the 7014960, on which the air meter was stamped 7014801 and cast 7014804, and the fuel meter was stamped 7014962 and cast 7014312.

The 1959 model year saw three injection units specified for 290bhp motor. First came the 7014900R, as used in '58. Second was the 7017250 with air meter stamped 7017251 and cast 7014922, and fuel meter stamped 7017252 and cast 7014889. Last was the 7017300, with air meter stamped 7017301 and cast 7014922, and fuel meter stamped 7017302, 7014802 or 7014965 and cast 7014312. Like the 7017300R, this was a recycled and re-calibrated unit made up from extra 7014800 units that

had not been used on the '57 Corvette or the '58 passenger car; they can correctly feature a diversity of parts. With the updating process, their original tags were removed and replaced by new tags identified by their over-sized rivets.

Both of the last two injection units were also used in '60. Additionally for this model year there was a 7017320 with air meter stamped 7017251 and cast 7014922, and fuel meter stamped 7017252 and cast 7014889. Once again it should be emphasized that further reading and discussion with a specialist is required before investing money in a Rochester fuel injection unit.

Other details remained as for the 250bhp unit, except that the tachometer was red-lined at 6500rpm and read to 8000rpm. Like the other solid lifter engine, the RPO 469C, this RPO 579D motor was also cooled in 1960 only by an aluminum Harrison radiator (part number 3147516) with the integral type of top tank.

It was intended that for 1960 the two RPO 579 fuel-injected engines would be given a performance boost by fitting them with aluminum cylinder heads. Not only would this have led to a substantial weight saving, but the better conductivity of the material would have allowed a higher compression ratio

without pre-ignition. The new compression ratio would have been 11.0:1, ideal to exploit the fuel injection's ability to deliver exactly the right mixture to each combustion chamber every time.

The aluminum heads were widely publicized, not least because they added 25bhp to the output of both fuel-injected motors, putting their power ratings at 275bhp and 315bhp respectively. They also had larger valves – the diameter of the intakes increased from 1.72in to 1.94in – and were allegedly manufactured without valve seat inserts, relying for hardness instead on the high silicon content of the aluminum alloy from which they were cast.

It seems that these aluminum heads were fitted to some early production 1960 fuel-injected models, but there were problems both with cracking of the heads and distortion following overheating, leading to blown head gaskets – rarely a problem with the cast iron heads. The decision was taken to revert to the cast iron head, returning power outputs to the previous year's levels. Opinions vary as to how many, if any, cars were sold with these aluminum heads, so any 1960 fuel-injected car found with original aluminum heads would now be an extremely rare piece. As it turned out, another 27 years would pass before Chevrolet again chanced aluminum heads on a production small-block V8.

The FOA 121 temperature-controlled radiator fan was an option only in 1960 and destined to be base equipment on all Corvettes from 1961 to 1982. The

In 1960 there were five different fuel injection units, of which three had ribbed plenums and two were plain, as on this 290bhp motor.

Unlike many fiberglass-bodied cars, Corvette's hidden parts such as this hood latch are stoutly designed and well fixed to the body. Ever increasing power output demanded better cooling, and this aluminum radiator with integral non-pressurized overflow tank by Harrison was supplied on 1960 270bhp carburetor and 290bhp injection cars.

ENGINE IDENTIFICATION

Engine block cast numbers

1958	283cu in (V8)	3737739 or 3756519
1959	283cu in (V8)	3737739 or 3756519
1960	283cu in (V8)	3756519

Stamped engine number suffixes

1958-60	283cu in (V8)	CQ	230bhp 1x4B carb manual
	283cu in (V8)	DG	230bhp 1x4B carb auto
	283cu in (V8)	CT	245bhp 2x4B carb manual
	283cu in (V8)	DJ	245bhp 2x4B carb auto
	283cu in (V8)	CR	250bhp injection manual
	283cu in (V8)	DH	250bhp injection auto
	283cu in (V8)	CU	270bhp 2x4B carb manual
	283cu in (V8)	CS	290bhp injection high-lift cam manual

temperature-sensitive fan clutch was promoted as allowing the fan to free-wheel when the engine was cool, saving power, fuel and belt wear. A more efficient five-blade fan was included. The real benefit turned out to be a reduction in under-hood noise. Just 2711 of this option were selected by customers out of total 1960 sales of 10,261.

Introduced in March 1959, the LPO 1625 24-gallon fuel tank was primarily a circuit racing accessory replacing both stock 17-gallon tank and the convertible top, whose storage space it also occupied. As a result, the tank could only be ordered with the RPO 419 auxiliary hard-top. Whereas the stock tank was made of pressed steel, the 24-gallon tank was made of fiberglass. The tank was required for longer circuit races where the standard tank would not carry sufficient fuel for a highly tuned engine doing as little as 5mpg at racing speeds.

ELECTRICS

For the three years 1958-60 the FOA 102 radio option was ordered by 66 per cent, 72 per cent and 79 per cent of buyers respectively, and the same seven-tube Wonder Bar AM signal-seeking radio – similar but not identical to the '57 version and with serial number 987730 – was used in each year. These are quite simple and reliable units, and can still be repaired to be enjoyed today.

As well as the radio receiver, the FOA 102 option comprised a number of other elements, none of which was fitted to non-radio cars. First was the loud-speaker and transformer assembly which fitted under the grille in the top of the dash. At the rear of the car a telescopic antenna was fitted in the top of the left fender, with a ground strap bolted to the frame to ensure good reception.

In dry weather AM reception is particularly prone to static interference, and to help prevent this static collectors were installed inside the front wheel grease caps to take the static charge to ground. Over the years, these have inevitably been discarded by mechanics – including myself, it must be admitted,

many years ago! – who did not know what they were. As with most cars of this era, radio interference capacitors were mounted on the generator, voltage regulator, coil and ammeter. Flexible woven metal ground straps were also used to connect the accelerator linkage to the intake manifold, the front engine mount bolts to the frame, and both exhaust pipes to the frame cross-member.

As with all radio-equipped Corvettes built before 1981, the distributor and ignition system were also shielded. The top shield was stainless steel and retained by hexagon-head bolts, apart from during early '58 production. The remainder of the shielding was chromium-plated steel and consisted of two vertical shields and two horizontal U-sections retained by wing nuts over each bank of plugs. Besides preventing interference from the spark plugs, the caps were also protected from the hot exhaust manifolds.

TRANSMISSION

Four-speed manual transmission may have been the sensation of 1957, but a solid 20 per cent of buyers continued to order the trusty automatic transmission (RPO 313). The two-speed cast iron Powerglide automatic was not available with the 270bhp or 290bhp solid lifter motors, or with Positraction axle.

The shift pattern will keep the modern driver alert. For the 1958 model year the previous (from front to back) R-L-D-N-P arrangement at first continued, but this was soon changed, in December 1957, to L-D-N-R-P. This pattern would remain until the beginning of '62 production when it was changed to the now conventional P-R-N-D-L with the introduction of the aluminum-cased Powerglide.

The iron-cased Saginaw three-speed manual gearbox remained the base transmission, but by this stage a majority of owners were opting to pay the extra $215.20 for the RPO 685 Borg Warner T-10 four-speed manual. Interestingly, the four-speed 'box shares the ratios of the three-speed – 2.2:1 low, 1.33:1 intermediate, 1:1 direct top – but has 1.66:1 inserted for second gear.

In 1959 a reverse lock-out T-bar was added to the four-speed shift lever, with a steel cable and stainless steel cable cover attached to the lever. The main case carried the cast identification T10-1 until mid-1959, when, following some internal improvements, the identification changed to T10-1B and remained through the end of 1960 production. In 1960 the clutch bellhousing was changed to aluminum.

The Positraction limited slip rear axle, available only with manual transmission, was a particularly useful option with the crude rear suspension and narrow tires of the time. On a wet road it is easy to spin one wheel with the standard axle, particularly on the original crossply tires. Available from 1957, the Positraction unit was a four-plate design until '61, when a five-plate version was adopted. Cars thus equipped carried a warning sticker on the spare wheel cover, to prevent in-gear engine operation with one wheel jacked – surely a stupid thing to do with any car, limited slip or not! This option was listed, according to axle ratio, as RPO 677, 678 or 679 in '58, but thereafter the code was RPO 675.

WHEELS & TIRES

The standard wheel covers on the '58 were unchanged from those introduced in '56, but now the wheels themselves were all painted silver instead of body color. For '59 the wheel covers were slightly redesigned to incorporate 10 oval cooling holes around their perimeter. The holes also allowed the escape of loose grit, which would otherwise be trapped and make a noise. Until the introduction of these holes, the spaces between the centre section of the wheel and the rim were filled with short lengths of rubber tube to prevent stray material entering.

Hubcaps varied year by year, and corresponded with the base Chevrolet passenger car items of the same year: the 1958 cap had three radial ribs, the '59 had six radial ribs, and the '60 cap was similar except for a depression pressed into the outer rim.

Ordering five 5.5in wide wheels (RPO 276) in place of the standard 5in wheels was the cheapest option of this period because it cost nothing. The substitution of small passenger car hubcaps for the full wheel covers with spinners compensated for the extra cost of the wider wheels; stock wheel covers would not fit. These wheels enabled the use of 7.10-15 or 7.60-15 tires, although stock 6.70-15 tires were supplied from the factory. Unlike the standard wheels, the wide wheels were painted black in '58 and '59, body color in '60.

SUSPENSION & STEERING

The suspension was an almost exact carryover from 1957, but detail changes were made after '58. Although the '58 was some 165lbs heavier than the '57, the spring rates were unchanged.

At the rear of late '57 cars a pair of bump stops had been introduced to limit the upper travel of the rear axle and spring, and this arrangement continued for '58, the front stop (part number 3731112) acting on the spring particularly to resist spring wind-up under hard acceleration, the rear stop (part number 3712357) acting on the axle. A significant improvement for '59 was the addition of a pair of rear axle control arms, which further assisted the springs in control of the axle and the prevention of wind-up under hard acceleration. At the same time the lower spring plate, through which the axle U-bolts passed, was strengthened where it turned down to support the shock absorber. This plate was common to the 1955-57 'Tri-Chevy' models, but unique to the

Manual four-speed shift with new reverse lock-out T-bar on a '59, still with adjacent ashtray on the console. If radio or heater were not ordered, then blanking plates were supplied.

Stock '59-62 hubcap with cooling slots around perimeter.

Unrestored heavy duty front brake, showing segmented lining, internal fan and cold air duct from intake behind right-hand front bumper.

Revised parking brake and hood release levers were found on 1958-60 models.

heavy probably for any enthusiast more used to later Corvettes with power steering. Also included were stiffer shock absorbers all round, stiffer front coil springs, an extra leaf in the rear springs, and a front sway bar of increased diameter (1³⁄₁₆in instead of 1¹⁄₁₆in). Positraction and manual transmission were also required when ordering this option.

BRAKES

While the standard front and rear brakes continued unchanged for '58, and conveniently even shared parts with the passenger cars, the braking elements of the Heavy Duty Brakes & Steering option (RPO 684) were further developed for the 144 customers who specified it that year. Either braking system used the same master cylinder (cast number 5450288 or 5456022) with a metal hexagon-headed filler cap.

RPO 684 could only be ordered in combination with one of the two 'special camshaft' engines: the 270bhp dual four-barrel carburetor 283 (RPO 469C) or the 290bhp 'Maximum Performance' fuel-injected version (RPO 579D). The principle and specification of RPO 684 was essentially the same as for the '57 version of this option (see page 53), but now advantage was taken of the additional openings below the quad headlamps. Rather than being left as a styling feature with no function, they were opened to admit cold air through a newly designed system of ducting to the rear brakes. Though normally partly obscured by the front bumpers, these openings became fully exposed when the bumpers were removed to save weight for circuit racing.

External air collected from the outer intakes was directed up over the front wheel within the arch in a well-hidden, molded duct. Behind the front wheel, this duct terminated in a round section to which was clamped a length of flexible ducting similar to the under-hood heater intake duct, and this in turn led through another duct into the rocker panel. Thereafter the arrangement was similar to the 1957 system. Later, in February 1958, a pair of front brake air scoops were provided at either end of the toothed center grille opening. These were not fitted on the assembly line, but were placed in the trunk with an instruction sheet for fitment by the dealer or owner.

In October 1958, after about 500 '59 model year cars had been built, the rear brake air ducting was removed and the price of the RPO 684 option was reduced by $354.95 to $425.05. At the same time the front brake scoops were swapped side to side, to drop them 2½in into the air stream and make them more effective – and this modification was recommended on earlier RPO 684 cars.

In the 1959 volume 2 number 4 edition of *Corvette News* came the recommendation that when an RPO 684 car was not being used on the track, the special shoes for its ceramic/metal brakes should be saved and replaced by non-Corvette passenger car components

Corvette thereafter when Chevrolet went to softer coil rear springing for its passenger cars.

A more minor modification for '59 affected the shock absorbers, which were changed to a plain pattern without a spiral in the lower body. For '60 the front sway bar was simplified by making it straight (not cranked) between the two frame insulators.

Though the brakes are the most important element of the optional RPO 684 (or RPO 687 for 1960) Heavy Duty Brakes & Steering, the package still included the bolt-on quick steering adapter which lengthened the center steering arm, and therefore its leverage, to change the steering ratio from 21:1 to 16.3:1. This reduced the turns lock to lock from 3.7 to 2.9, and, of course, made the steering heavier – too that would fit the wider finned drum. This would, of course, make the car safer to drive when the brakes were cold – but this whole scenario is unthinkable in today's litigious atmosphere! It follows that today's owner should preserve and display his race shoes, and save those valuable drums by driving on road shoes.

Acknowledging the shortcomings of the brakes for the performance-minded road driver, Special Brake Linings (RPO 686) were introduced for a meagre $26.90 and taken up by 333 buyers of '59s. Of sintered metallic composition, these came with heat-resistant return springs and specially honed but standard-sized brake drums. This option was restricted to manual transmission cars.

The designation of the Heavy Duty Brakes & Suspension option changed from RPO 684 to RPO 687 for 1960, but the specification continued as for late '59 with the exception that pressed steel 24-vane cooling fans were installed in all four brake drums to circulate cooling air, and mesh-covered cooling apertures were cut into the front brake backing plates. Instead of the ceramic linings, sintered metal was now used, still arranged in segments; this was the same material used for RPO 686 but the shoes were wider. The ceramic/metal linings were still recommended as a 'service replacement...for competitive events'.

The parking brake alarm (FOA 107), which had been standard before 1956 but then became optional, now had the previous large red warning lamp replaced by a discreet flashing red 'brake' warning in the speedometer face.

OPTIONS

Many options have been discussed through this chapter, but the full list of options available for the 1958, '59 and '60 model years is given in the accompanying panel.

OPTIONS

1958

Code	Option	Quantity	Price
–	1958 Corvette Convertible	9168	$3591.00
Standard	283/230bhp	5487	No cost
FOA 101	Heater	8014	$96.85
FOA 102	Wonder Bar radio	6142	$144.45
FOA 107	Parking brake alarm	1873	$5.40
FOA 108	Courtesy lights	4600	$6.50
FOA 109	Windshield washers	3834	$16.15
RPO 276	15x5.5in wheels	404	No cost
RPO 290	6.70x15 whitewall tires	7428	$31.55
RPO 313	Powerglide automatic	2057	$188.30
RPO 419	Auxiliary hard-top	5607	$215.20
RPO 426	Power windows	649	$59.20
RPO 440	Two-tone paint	3422	$16.15
RPO 469	245bhp 2x4B carb motor	2436	$150.65
RPO 469C	270bhp 2x4B carb motor	978	$182.95
RPO 470	White or blue-gray soft-top	4622	No cost
RPO 473	Power convertible top	1090	$139.90
RPO 579A	250bhp fuel injection manual	400	$484.20
RPO 579B	250bhp fuel injection auto	104	$484.20
RPO 579D	290bhp fuel injection	1007	$484.20
RPO 677	3.70:1 Positraction	1123	$48.45
RPO 678	4.11:1 Positraction	2518	$48.45
RPO 679	4.56:1 Positraction	370	$48.45
RPO 684	Heavy Duty Brakes & Suspension	144	$780.10
RPO 685	Four-speed T-10 transmission	3764	$215.20

1959

Code	Option	Quantity	Price
–	Corvette convertible	9670	$3875.00
Standard	283/230bhp	4243	No cost
FOA 101	Heater	8909	$102.25
FOA 102	Wonder Bar radio	7001	$149.80
FOA 107	Parking brake alarm	3601	$5.40
FOA 108	Courtesy lights	4600	$6.50
FOA 109	Windshield washers	7929	$16.15
RPO 121	Clutch, radiator fan	67	$21.55
RPO 261	Sun visors	3722	$10.80
RPO 276	15x5.5in wheels	214	No cost
RPO 290	6.70x15 whitewall tires	8173	$31.55
RPO 313	Powerglide automatic	1878	$199.10
RPO 419	Auxiliary hard-top	5481	$236.75
RPO 426	Power windows	587	$59.20
RPO 440	Two-tone paint	2931	$16.15
RPO 469	245bhp 2x4B carb motor	1417	$150.65
RPO 469C	270bhp 2x4B carb motor	1846	$182.95
RPO 470	White or blue-gray soft-top	4721	No cost
RPO 473	Power convertible top	661	$139.90
RPO 579A	250bhp fuel injection manual	141	$484.20
RPO 579B	250bhp fuel injection auto	34	$484.20
RPO 579D	290bhp fuel injection	745	$484.20
RPO 675	3.70:1 Positraction	1362	$48.45
	4.11:1 Positraction	2523	$48.45
	4.56:1 Positraction	285	$48.45
RPO 684	Heavy Duty Brakes & Suspension	142	$425.05
RPO 685	Four-speed T-10 transmission	4175	$188.30
RPO 686	Metallic brakes	333	$26.90
LPO 1408	6.70x15in nylon tires	–	–
LPO 1625	24-gallon fuel tank	–	–

1960

Code	Option	Quantity	Price
–	Corvette convertible	10263	$3872.00
Standard	283/230bhp	5827	No cost
FOA 101	Heater	9809	$102.25
FOA 102	Wonder Bar radio	8166	$137.75
FOA 107	Parking brake alarm	4051	$5.40
FOA 108	Courtesy lights	6774	$6.50
FOA 109	Windshield washers	7205	$16.15
RPO 121	Clutch, radiator fan	2711	$21.55
RPO 261	Sun visors	5276	$10.80
RPO 276	15x5.5in wheels	246	No cost
RPO 290	6.70x15 whitewall tires	9104	$31.55
RPO 313	Powerglide automatic	1766	$199.10
RPO 419	Auxiliary hard-top	5147	$236.75
RPO 426	Power windows	544	$59.20
RPO 440	Two-tone paint	3309	$16.15
RPO 469	245bhp 2x4B carb motor	1211	$150.65
RPO 469C	270bhp 2x4B carb motor	2364	$182.95
RPO 470	White or blue soft-top	5380	No cost
RPO 473	Power convertible top	512	$139.90
RPO 579	250bhp fuel injection	100	$484.20
RPO 579D	290bhp fuel injection	759	$484.20
RPO 675	3.70:1 Positraction	1548	$43.05
	4.11:1 Positraction	3226	$43.05
	4.56:1 Positraction	457	$43.05
RPO 685	Four-speed T-10 transmission	5328	$188.30
RPO 686	Metallic brakes	920	$26.90
RPO 687	Heavy Duty Brakes & Suspension	119	$333.60
LPO 1408	6.70x15 nylon tires	–	–
LPO 1625	24-gallon fuel tank	–	$161.40

1961-1962

By 1960 Chevrolet were committed to the Sting Ray design for the '63 Corvette and needed a gradual transition towards it for the '61-62 models. The new four-lamp tail achieved this. The tail design still causes disagreement among enthusiasts about the success of its aesthetics.

DIMENSIONS

Length	17.70in
Width	70.4in
Height	52.2in
Wheelbase	102in
Max track	59in
Curb weight (auto)	3135lbs

After three years of the same shape of Corvette, and two years of models that could not be distinguished from each other at a glance, the time was ripe for a change. By April 1960 the external design of the radically different, all-independent suspension Sting Ray had been finalised, but to allow time to ready this model for production the launch was scheduled for fall 1962.

In eight years of production the Corvette had become an extraordinary success in every area except sales. Facing the axe after its uncertain first three years, it had probably been saved by Ford's introduction of the Thunderbird, and, as explained earlier, GM management were not going to surrender a market sector of their invention to their arch rivals, who examined the Corvette and then improved upon it. The T-Bird was such a staggering success that in 1960 it sold 92,798 units against the Corvette's 10,261. It can be assumed that the Ford product was very profitable, but the Corvette, with its largely hand-built body, was only marginally profitable at best. The T-Bird, however, was by now a slushy four-seater and even looked old-fashioned compared with its 1960 full-sized sisters – and only 11,860 of the 1960 T-Birds were convertibles.

The success of the Corvette was in emphasizing to the world at large that Chevrolet was now a performance brand, with the Corvette its technological showcase. The 283cu in small-block was now the outstanding performance motor, which could be enhanced by fuel injection, and had numerous race wins to its credit. Eighth place at the Le Mans 24-hour endurance race in 1960 in a basically standard car driven by John Fitch and Bob Grossman was an outstanding achievement, and has yet to be improved on by the many Corvette entries since.

The Corvette's fiberglass body was also proving to be popular with owners. The styling was still superb, and the extra headlamps, larger chromium-plated bumpers and more aggressive styling fitted in well with most of the cars that you would have seen downtown or at the drive-in in the pre-mall year of 1960. From 1956 the body had also looked as though it were made from futuristic materials, and Corvettes have never suffered from the wavy panels that characterized many of the smaller European plastic-bodied cars whose panels were hand-laid into female molds rather than pressed between matched dies.

Those who could bother to read the Shop Manual would also find an excellent eight-page section on repairing fiberglass, including instructions on the correct preparation of the hands with part-numbered

barrier creams before starting work with the GM kits – Plastic Solder for minor repairs or the Resin Repair Kit for the larger job.

Sting Ray production in 1963 would be double that of the '60 Corvette, and the transition was carefully orchestrated. The styling of the '63 was based on Bill Mitchell's Sting Ray Racer of 1959 that had won the SCCA C-Modified National Championship in its class in 1960. This was a Dream Car that won races, and now the 1953 scenario of Dream Car to production car could be repeated ten years later.

The rear of the Sting Ray Racer was more race car than road car, but another dream car, the XP-700, had already featured a more production-ready tail with trunk and lights, and a version of this was incorporated into the 1961 Corvette. Thus the continuity of the Corvette look would be maintained, so that those seeing the '63 for the first time, particularly from the rear, would know immediately what it was.

The second major change over this period was the transition for 1962 to an all-new line-up of 327cu in engines which would carry over almost unchanged to the new '63, thereby simplifying the new model introduction. The same tactics would be used for the 1967-68 and 1982-84 changeovers, though not for the 1996-97.

The cleaner lines of the last two years of 'straight-axle' production appealed to a new generation and marked the beginnings of Bill Mitchell's reign, which had commenced with the retirement of Harley Earl in 1958 and would last 20 years, eventually leading to General Motors producing some of the most beautiful designs ever. It has been said that GM built over 100 million cars that had been styled by Mitchell and his team.

While the rear body was different for '61 and '62, the majority of the body panels and other components were the same as they had been since '56, while the frame and suspension dated back to '53. This was a two-year period when the car was further refined, while Chevrolet could at last enjoy some profit as their investment in tooling became amortized. Indeed, for 1962 a second shift was introduced for the first time at the Corvette section of the St Louis plant and production increased to 14,531 – the Corvette's best year thus far.

BODY & TRIM

From the front, the most obvious change for 1961 was the replacement of the grille teeth by a plain anodized aluminum mesh with 14 horizontal bars. The

Front end was updated, too, by discarding grille teeth, adding chrome name letters and crossed flags, and painting headlamp bezels body color.

Hard-top was different at rear due to need to accommodate central rib on rear deck lid and trunk lid; 1961 was the last year for stainless steel cove surround and tires with wide whitewalls.

chromium-plated center crossbar used for 1961-62 (part number 3779661) was smaller than the 1958-60 version and lacked the holes for mounting the teeth. This in turn meant that the main front bumpers for 1961-62 were different at their inner ends from the previous year's. The upper and lower chromium-plated cast main grille shells had different part numbers but the same fit as 1958-60.

The 1962 grille was a slightly different pressing from the '61 but more importantly was finished in black. From time to time there have been suggestions that some '62s may have had gold anodized grilles, even to identify high-performance options, but it is now generally accepted that this rather appealing finish was never supplied on new cars. The black grille did not look out of place because it now matched the black areas within the two outer false grilles.

Also new for 1961-62 was a shorter pair of front bumperette support brackets. If these brackets are missing, the normally available replacement is the 1960 or earlier version, which was longer because the license plate and bumperette assembly had to clear the grille teeth. If fitted, these brackets will make the assembly stand out too far for the correct appearance – not a disadvantage if the car is to be regularly used on the road as it should be.

Further refining the frontal appearance was a new emblem to replace the previous three-piece assembly which had fitted into a hole in the bodywork. Now a crossed-flag motif (part number 3781030), unique to the front of the '61 model, was fitted to the center of the front panel above the seven individual letters C-O-R-V-E-T-T-E, which were also used for '62.

Finishing the front-end facelift, the headlamp bezels, which had previously been chromium-plated, were now painted body color, resulting in a more integrated appearance. A new bright metal molding, called a fender molding extension (part number 3779240), was riveted to the bezel to retain the visual effect of the fender top trim starting between the pairs of headlamps.

Behind the front wheel opening, the cove with its stainless steel surround and triple spears was unchanged, but the crossed-flag emblem was replaced for '61 by a three-piece unit comprising a plate with CORVETTE in upper case letters (part number 3779671) flanked by a horizontal chromium ornament with red infill (part numbers 3779673 left, 3779674 right) above and a similar ornament with blue infill (part numbers 3779675 left and 3779676 right) below.

Behind the doors all the panels were new, the arris

Removing the stainless steel cove surround required new fenders and doors for the '62, but the new tail, helped by the new bright rocker molding, now seemed better integrated with the rest of the car. Black front grille and front fender grilles were also new for '62. Wheels were black with white-wall tires, otherwise body color.

which defined the rear of the car extending over the rear wheel openings. Proving that Chevrolet did not mind making life difficult for themselves and their parts people in years to come, a styled rib or wind-split was introduced running from the front of the deck lid to the rear of the new trunk lid. Devotees of Mitchell style will at once recognize this as one of his trademarks: a similar rib adorned the rear of all 1963-67 Sting Rays and the 1971-72 Buick Riviera boat tail, among others. That this also necessitated a revised hard-top and soft-top to accommodate the rib was evidence of the sway that Mitchell held, and his laudable determination to get every detail right at any cost. It can be annoying that a 1961-62 replacement

convertible top cannot be fitted to a 1960 car, but the design was undoubtedly improved by that rib.

The new wind-split rear deck molding forced two changes to the design of the optional hard-top (RPO 419), and more than half of 1961-62 buyers opted either to take a hard-top instead of a convertible top or pay an extra $236.75 to have both. The fixing system at the rear was changed from three to two bolts because of the loss of the third central position to the wind-split, but at the rear of the door opening were two additional brackets (instead of the previous locating pins) so that the hard-top mounting was improved overall. Like the convertible top, the hard-top back window and rear bow were reshaped to fit

Hard-top was either a no-cost substitution for the soft-top or a $236.75 extra if both tops were required. Without a folding top, the space liberated could be used for extra bags (accessed by lifting the front of the hard-top and deck lid as a unit) or extra gas capacity (by ordering the 24-gallon fuel tank).

the new central rib. Hard-tops were supplied only in colors to match the interior and exterior of the car.

When a Corvette was supplied with a hard-top only, the mounting brackets and outer panel reinforcements to which the brackets were fixed were omitted. A washer was used as a spacer beneath the seat belt mounting bracket, so that this mounted square without the reinforcement in place. It must be assumed that the reinforcement was omitted as a cost-saving measure. In the Corvette's transition from everyday to classic car status, a car with only a hard-top loses some of its appeal, particularly in parts of the world with weather less certain than that of southern California. There is no doubt that the folding roof

adds to the enjoyment of the car. To find a good original convertible top and frame is tough, although good and usable reproductions are now available – but to have the top and then discover that the brackets are missing from the car is really frustrating.

The convertible top had a redesigned rear bow, now aluminum, to accommodate the rib in the deck. Color choice for the top fabric was now restricted to black or white.

The appeal of the less than satisfying powered folding top option (RPO 473), unchanged for the last two years of production, continued to diminish. In 1961 fewer than 4 per cent of buyers chose to spend the extra $161.40, and this declined to less than 3 per

Comparative views of a pair of '62 models. Sateen Silver car, with hard-top, has optional 5.5in wheels with blackwall tires. Fawn Beige car has white convertible top and narrow whitewall tires – with ⅞in wide band – first seen that year.

Painted headlamp surrounds on '61 required a separate pointed end for the top spear, which had previously blended into the single chromed bezel for the paired headlamps. Apart from rear lamps that predicted Sting Ray styling, rear end featured exhaust that discharged discreetly behind rear wheel – no more corroded bumpers, but downward-facing pipe blows up dust instead.

Emblems on front (right) and rear (far right) of '61 Corvette. Gold lettering on rear badge faded over the years to silver, prompting endless discussion as to whether any were originally silver. The answer is no… probably!

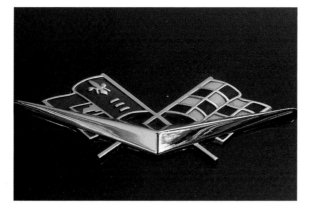

Emblems on front (right) and rear (far right) of '62 Corvette. Both were unique to the model year, the dark background on the rear badge refreshing a design that dated from 1958.

Differing badges on the stylized vent behind the front wheel: logo with colored bars replaced the previous crossed flags, while 'fuel injection' motif was unique to appropriate '62 cars.

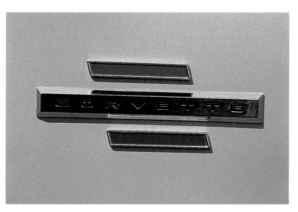

cent in 1962 despite a $21.50 price reduction. Compared with the outstanding and complex Ford Skyliners and other conventional power tops that had been seen since 1956, the Corvette system lacked the power latches that would make it fully automatic, and these were probably judged inappropriate for a sports car. Chevrolet would not put a power top on a Corvette for the next 35 years.

Rear bumpers were entirely new and did not risk damage from the exhaust, whose outlets now terminated unobtrusively downward behind the rear wheels. Unobtrusive but not without style, the outlet pipe of the exhaust was slash-cut on a curve to give a flared effect; a straight pipe at this point is often seen but looks quite wrong to the enthusiast. The bumpers were not as long at the sides of the car and finished well short of the wheel openings. Around the rear license plate opening there was a new central bumper

in the form of an inverted U to complete the arrangements for rear protection.

It may be recalled from the previous chapter that the large 1958-60 rear bumper had to be fitted after the body had been dropped on to the chassis, whereas until 1957 the bumpers had been fitted prior to the body drop. Careful examination of the few published photographs of 1961-62 production suggest that, for these two years only, all three rear bumper elements were also fitted prior to body drop, but that the front bumper was fitted afterwards.

The four rear lamps started an enduring Corvette tradition that looks set to continue into the next century. The lenses (part number 5954803) were continued through to the end of Sting Ray production in 1967, but the four chromium-plated cast housings (part numbers 899629-30 outer, 899630-31 inner) were unique to these two years. The fact that

COLORS

1961

Body	Cove option	Wheels	Soft-top	Interior
Tuxedo Black	Silver	As body	Black or White	Black, Blue, Red or Fawn
Ermine White	Silver	As body	Black or White	Black, Blue, Red or Fawn
Roman Red	White	As body	Black or White	Black or Red
Sateen Silver	White	As body	Black or White	Black, Blue or Red
Jewel Blue	White	As body	Black or White	Black or Blue
Fawn Beige	White	As body	Black or White	Black, Red or Fawn
Honduras Maroon	White	As body	Black or White	Black or Fawn

1962

Body	Cove option	Wheels	Soft-top	Interior
Tuxedo Black	–	As body	Black or White	Black, Red or Fawn
Fawn Beige	–	As body	Black or White	Red or Fawn
Roman Red	–	As body	Black or White	Black, Red or Fawn
Ermine White	–	As body	Black or White	Black, Red or Fawn
Almond Beige	–	As body	Black or White	Red or Fawn
Sateen Silver	–	As body	Black or White	Black or Red
Honduras Maroon	White	As body	Black or White	Black or Fawn

Visibility was excellent with the auxiliary hard-top, an option since 1956, but two people were needed to fit or remove it.

these lamps protruded into the interior of the trunk at floor level made the sockets and wiring prone to damage from loose luggage, so in 1962 plastic tail light protector cones were fitted to solve this problem. While incorrect on a '61, they provide worthwhile protection and can easily be removed when concours judging looms.

The final facelift for the Corvette for '62 saw the complete removal of the brightwork around the cove and the dual color option. Instead the cove shape was subtly molded into the fiberglass of the door and front fender, a treatment that matched the revised rear end particularly well. The effect was emphasized by an aluminum sill molding below the door and a new cove vent insert to replace the spears of the previous four years. The finish of this molding was entirely bright aluminum for approximately the first 3000 '62 models, but after this indeterminate point its fluted recesses were painted black.

As well as the black intake grille, a 1962-only crossed flag inside a circle (part number 3796355) was fitted above the CORVETTE letters at the front, while the only change at the rear was to make the backing bowl of the emblem black rather than the silver used from 1958. There is considerable doubt as to the correct color of the lettering on this emblem. Officially it was changed to silver for 1962, but there is evidence that many '62s left the factory with gold lettering, as in previous years.

Early publicity from the volume 3 number 4 issue of Chevrolet's own *Corvette News*, published in the fall of 1960, suggested that the crude and not very effective pulley and cable windshield wiper operation would be replaced by a positive rod linkage, but this was not to be and the system remained as before. The reader will have realized by now that the writer is strongly in favor of using Corvettes of any age as often as possible, but it must be said that the wipers of the straight-axle are at best inadequate. Fitch and Grossman's eighth place at Le Mans was said to have owed a lot to the ability of the narrow-tired and heavy Corvette to cut through the standing water in one of the wettest 24-hour races ever, but it is hard to see how they ever coped with those wipers.

The 1962 model year was the last appearance for the wraparound windshield with forward-sloping pillars. In 1953 the Corvette had been the first production car to use this style and it had gone on to be featured on millions of GM cars and copied by others both at home and world-wide. Now the '62 Corvette had the distinction of also being the last built with the wraparound windshield.

CHASSIS

Following the improvements to the chassis that had already occurred, the two rear axle location bars in '59 and the rear sway bar in '60, no refinements were scheduled for 1961-62. The new 1963 Sting Ray would boast state-of-the-art all-round independent suspension, so there was little to achieve by tampering with the existing set-up, which was as ready as it could ever be to handle the extra torque and power promised for 1961.

CHASSIS NUMBERS

1961	10867S100001 – 10867S110939
1962	20867S100001 – 20867S114531

INTERIOR

For 1961 the interior continued much as before. At the same time as the new rear outer panels were introduced, the rear under-body was revised to provide more internal room by reducing the width of the transmission tunnel. The sill or step plate was now

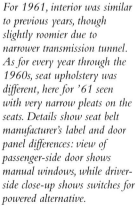

For 1961, interior was similar to previous years, though slightly roomier due to narrower transmission tunnel. As for every year through the 1960s, seat upholstery was different, here for '61 seen with very narrow pleats on the seats. Details show seat belt manufacturer's label and door panel differences: view of passenger-side door shows manual windows, while driver-side close-up shows switches for powered alternative.

formed as a single piece rather than in two pieces, and the two-piece filler beneath it was Masonite instead of hardwood. The spare wheel cover was still plywood, and this would be the last structural use of forest products in the Corvette until the balsa wood filling for the floor of the 1997 model.

Beginning with 1961, sun visors became standard rather than the optional equipment they had been since '59. While the 1961 sun visor was mounted in the same way as the 1959-60, the 1962 nuts and screws were fitted so that the head of the screw was visible with the sun visor raised, rather than the nut visible as had been the case previously.

Seat patterns also changed for '61 with much finer pleats on the seat inserts, which stopped well short of

the front of the seat. For '62 the number of pleats was reduced and the pleating taken over the top of the seat back. The seat mounting in the floor was also modified, allowing the runners to be refitted further back to permit more leg room, although the Corvette remained inhospitable to the taller driver. By '62 the length of the steering column, which had not been much changed since '56, now seemed to put the wheel awfully close to the driver's chest.

Door panels for '61 were similar to the '60 except that the bright metal areas featured a horizontal stripe pattern instead of dimples. In line with the general loss of reflective metal, these were replaced altogether for the final year of production, and an entirely new panel with vertical pleats of vinyl – matching the seat

pattern – was used. The reflectors were also repositioned so that they were now mounted one above the other instead of in line with the arm rest. The arm rest, too, changed to the same 4332259 item that would be used in '63 and '64 Sting Rays. A new interior color, Fawn, replaced Turquoise for '61, and Blue was dropped for '62.

From the beginning of '62, the seat separator lid between the seats no longer carried the paint caution sticker that had been stuck there to warn of the changeover to acrylic paint since the beginning of '58 production. The interior rear-view mirror used the same base (part number 3747942) common to all 1958-62 Corvettes, but the mirror head was now styled so that its short sides were angled inward.

The redesign of the rear end, and the smoothing of the rear contours, led to a 20 per cent increase in the size of the trunk. More importantly, the opportunity was taken while reworking the rear panels to incorporate molded recesses to the left of the spare wheel in the trunk floor for the wheel wrench and the jack handle. They were thus neatly concealed by the rubber trunk mat and prevented from sliding about or scratching bags; previously there had been rather ineffective spring clips to retain these items either side of the trunk. Such neat details cost so little and add so much, and of all subsequent models only the '84, with its radiator shroud recess for the jack handle, has been comparable.

The heater (FOA 101) continued exactly as for previous years except for a change to the control knobs to match the rest of the dashboard (see below). In '62 the heater became standard equipment unless deleted under RPO 610. The knobs on the Wonder Bar radio (FOA 102) also changed in '61, from solid cast plastic to pressed metal, and there were minor changes to match the revised dashboard details. As

Final interior upgrades before new Sting Ray brought sunshades as standard equipment from 1961, but they are seen on a '62 model. Changes for that year, which set a new production record of 14,531 cars sold, included another variation in seat pleating and all-new door panels with arm rests that were shared with the '63-64 Sting Ray.

After '62, a trunk would not be seen again on a Corvette for 36 years! When redesigning the underbody to fit the new tail, Chevrolet engineers took the opportunity to incorporate molded cavities for the jack handle and wheel nut wrench; labels on spare wheel cover are Positraction warning (upper) and jacking instructions (lower). Protector cones were slipped over the exposed lamp units for '62 to save them from being damaged by loose items in the trunk. Instrument cluster introduced in 1958 still looked great; speedo needle obscures left-turn signal warning lamp when stationary. Radio and shifter consoles were essentially unchanged; radio push buttons were formed of stamped steel for '61-62 rather than cast as previously.

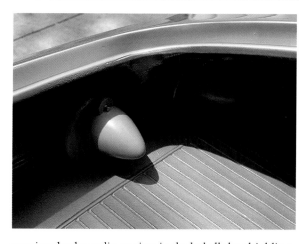

previously, the radio option included all the shielding, ground straps and the antenna. If no radio was ordered – 10 per cent of '62 buyers did not want one – all the other equipment was omitted as well.

INSTRUMENTS & CONTROLS

The instruments were unchanged except for the detail of a late 1962 alteration to the temperature gauge from a 220° F to 240° F maximum figure. The tachometer for '61 continued as for '60, but for '62 the base-model tachometer was driven from the distributor instead of the generator, and therefore had different internal gearing because the distributor runs at half engine speed. The parking brake warning lamp

in the speedometer became a standard rather than optional item, and was flashed by the use of a flashing 357 bulb instead of by a separate unit.

The headlamp, windshield wiper and other control knobs were given a new machined finish. The white plastic knob on the turn signal lever was changed in shape from a lozenge to an inverted cone with external fluting.

Although covered in the transmission section, it is worth noting here that 1962 was the year in which the Corvette adopted a conventional P-R-N-D-L automatic shift selector pattern, where the P was towards the front of the car; since mid-1958 the positions had been in reversed sequence. There are obviously good safety reasons to justify updating to the modern pattern on earlier cars.

ENGINES

Because the engine size and option numbers all changed for 1962, it is easier to examine the '61 and '62 model years separately.

The base 1961 283 motor was again a 230bhp and carried over almost entirely unchanged from 1960 (see pages 64-65). Apart from the first 1700 230bhp, 245bhp and 250bhp cars produced, however, all '61 Corvettes were fitted with an aluminum radiator and aluminum header tank. Filling was via a pressurized cap on the tank, which was bracket-mounted to the left side of the motor.

It is interesting that all new cars sold in California from 1961 had to have a Positive Crankcase Ventilation (PCV) system, and this applied to all states from 1963. It has been said of the American people that they not only discover the problems of modern civilization first, but also go on to invent the solutions. It was in southern California that photo-chemical smog was first noticed and analyzed. The vapour content of automotive crankcases was found to be a major constituent of the problem. Under the effect of the constantly varying volume, because of the action of the pistons, they were ventilated out of the engine through the road draft tube.

On the Corvette the PCV valve, ordered as RPO 242, was fitted between an adapter, which replaced the draft tube behind the distributor, and a fitting into the carburetor base or into the fuel injection plenum. This 1961-62 only PCV system is now a very rare part to find.

This was the humble beginning of the emissions equipment, which for the next 20 years would progressively dominate under-hood developments and restrict performance until the power of the on-board computer was harnessed in 1982, to increase rather than reduce power with every federally mandated reduction in emissions.

Engine options for '61 started with the RPO 469. This dual-carburetor engine was rated at 245bhp and was a carryover 1960 motor of the same option number. It was essentially a 230bhp motor with two carburetors mounted on an aluminum manifold (cast 3739653) and fitted with aluminum valve covers. See page 67 for details of this option.

Previously known in 1960 as RPO 469C, the Duntov camshaft and solid valve lifter 270bhp version of RPO 469 changed designation to RPO 468. It was otherwise identical (see page 67).

The next 1961 choice was the fuel-injected RPO 353 (also known as RPO 579) 275bhp. At the beginning of 1960 a new high-compression aluminum cylinder head had been proudly announced and this was to boost the power of the two injected motors by 25bhp, to 275bhp and 315bhp respectively. The aluminum head proved troublesome, however, and it is uncertain whether any made it as far as the show-room before they were withdrawn.

These heads were subsequently recast in iron (with cast number 3782461) and used with great success to achieve the eighth place at Le Mans in June 1960. They featured larger 1.94in intake valves with 1.5in exhaust valves and improved porting for better gas flow; combustion chamber volume was 62cc, giving a compression ratio of 11:1. With 'camel hump' or 'double bump' end identification, these heads, which were used through 1964, were the legendary fuelie heads so sought-after by hot rodders. The briefly available aluminum heads had the same cast number and are extremely rare.

For the first time, domed rather than flat-topped pistons were used with this motor. They were cast aluminum with machined valve clearance reliefs and a 0.060 pin offset. The Rochester injection unit used with this 275bhp engine was the flat-topped 7017310 or possibly the ribbed 7017200. Only 118 were sold and, with the inevitable removal and replacement over years, there is now some doubt as to what was original with such a small sample to research. The air cleaner was the same cold air unit that had been introduced in 1958.

Exhaust manifolds (cast 3750556) were the same as carburetor engines, but because the fuel injection's cold start was electrically controlled there was no requirement for the choke heat tube on the right-hand manifold. A spacer was also used instead of the heat riser valve, which was not required in this instance because there was no cross-over passage in the fuel injection intake manifold.

Following the increase in power, this engine was no longer available with automatic transmission. All 1961 fuel-injected Corvettes carried a pair of 'fuel injection' emblems (part number 3746457) on their front fenders.

Top engine option for 1961 was RPO 354 (also known as RPO 582). It is hard to see why in 1961 the 315bhp RPO 354 should outsell the 275bhp RPO 353 by a factor of more than ten to one, but perhaps this was a consequence of both options being priced at $484.20 – and who was going to turn down 40 free horsepower, even if torque was down to 295lb ft at a rather lofty 4700rpm?

The horsepower was achieved by combining the Duntov mechanical lifter camshaft with the new 3782461 big-valve 11:1 compression ratio heads. Pistons were the domed items used in the 275bhp, and the cylinder block was the same cast number 3756519 unit as the base engine.

This was the fastest and most powerful Corvette motor yet. The 315bhp output was sufficient to accelerate the 3080lb car through 0-60mph in 5.5secs, 0-100mph in 14.5secs and the standing quarter-mile in 14.2secs. While rival manufacturers Ford and Chrysler had more powerful power plants available, they were big-block designs in heavy cars that could never match the Corvette's agility. More cubic inches, however, were on the way for the 1962.

Fuel injection units for '61 were generally ribbed for the 275bhp motor but plain for the 315bhp unit. All of these engines used an aluminum radiator with a pressurized aluminum header tank attached to the left side of the motor. In '61 the generator drove the tachometer on the 275bhp motor, but not the 315bhp

The small-block engine was offered in 1962 Chevrolet passenger cars in an alternative larger 327cu in size and this was adopted as the basic Corvette block for the next seven years.

The cylinder bore was increased by ⅛in to 4in and the block was cast numbered 3782870, a figure that would see service until the end of 1965 production. The 4in bore was destined to continue in the cast iron small-block to the end of 1996 production, a run of 34 years. Care has to be taken when re-boring this block because of its thin cylinder walls, particularly on a 'matching numbers' engine.

The throw of the crankshaft was increased so that the stroke lengthened to 3¼in, making this the most over-square Corvette motor of all. Indeed, it often seems that a good 327 is the most delightful of small-blocks, arguably smoother and more willing to rev than the longer-stroke 350 that followed in 1969. Conveniently, the rod and bearing sizes of the 1962 327 were the same as on the 283 it replaced.

The standard 327 engine had 250bhp, 20bhp more than the '61 unit, the greater swept volume helping to push the compression ratio up to 10.5:1; pistons were cast flat-top. Air cleaner was the familiar 14in aluminum two-piece type with serviceable element. Two different Carter WCFB carburetors were used: 3190S with automatic transmission, 3191S with manual. The intake manifold was iron (cast number 3783244), and valve covers were stamped steel with a rectangular raised label area bearing the three-line transfer 'Chevrolet 327 Turbofire'.

Cylinder head for the 250bhp only was the 3795896 with 1.72in intake valves. With its small 59.67cc combustion chambers, this was known as the Powerpack head and continued in the 250bhp application through 1964. Exhaust manifolds were 2in outlet with cast numbers 3749965 (left) and 3750556 (right). The distributor was a 1110984 with vacuum advance and, for the first time on a base engine, it drove the tachometer.

Optional engines for 1962 started with the RPO 583 300bhp. Uniquely among 1956-62 optional engines, RPO 583 valve covers were stamped steel rather than cast aluminum, the ribbed covers now being reserved for the top two engine options. Topped by the usual aluminum 14in louvered air cleaner, the new larger Carter aluminum four-barrel (AFB) carburetor (3310S with Powerglide, 3269S for manual) was mounted on a cast iron intake manifold (3799349), a high-performance design also used on 300bhp passenger cars. This carburetor replaced the dual fours of the previous years, and these were not used again on Corvettes.

Cylinder heads were the 3782461 large-valve fuelie heads introduced in 1961, and exhaust manifolds were 3797901 (left) and 3797902 (right). These

The 340bhp of '62 used a single Carter AFB carburetor, engines with dual four-barrel carburetors having finished in 1961. Capacity on all four available engines for '62 was raised to 327cu in, a size that would be carried over to the new Sting Ray for '63.

The '62 fuel injection motor was rated at 360bhp – the most powerful fitted to a straight-axle car and one of the most desirable Corvette specifications ever.

2½in high-performance manifolds were also used on the other optional 1962 engines and were combined with 2½in exhaust pipes and cross-over pipes.

Continuing the new 327 range of engines was the RPO 396 340bhp, the most powerful carburetor engine yet. The first Corvette engine with a carburetor to exceed the 1957 benchmark of one horsepower per cubic inch, it was a bargain at $107.60 and proved to be the most popular optional engine of 1962. It was essentially an RPO 583 fitted with solid-lifter camshaft and domed forged pistons, giving an impressive 11.25:1 compression ratio – which today means that this engine requires modification before it can be used with modern fuels. The carburetor was mounted on a new 3795397 aluminum intake manifold unique to this year and application. Valve covers were also aluminum. The distributor was dual-point with centrifugal advance only and tachometer drive.

Top-of-the-line motor for the '62, and king of all straight-axle power options, was the RPO 582 fuel injection. This consisted of a 340bhp RPO 396 with Rochester fuel injection fitted instead of the carburetor and manifold. Early production used the 7017355 injection unit, but this was later superseded by a 7017360.

At 360bhp this motor, the only fuel-injected option for '62, was a full 50 per cent more powerful than the top optional engine of '56, and only 30bhp short of double the output of the first V8. The chassis had not changed very much, however, and this power now needed to be used with care, but again these motors were to be ideal for the sophisticated Sting Ray that was only a year away. Someone once said that the power of a sports car should exceed the capability of its chassis by 20 per cent if it is to be fun to drive – the RPO 582 fuel-injected Corvette could have been the car he had in mind!

A final word about a new option for '62. Stock Corvette mufflers were of a reverse-flow oval section design, but in 1962 a direct-flow system (RPO 441) was offered as a no-cost option for the first time and it is probable that the mufflers used were round in section. Because mufflers are the first part to be replaced due to rust, it is hard today to know what they looked like when they left the factory. Original literature refers to them as 'straight-through' and advises that they 'may also be used in normal driving where local regulations allow'. A total of 2934 owners of '62s either must have been racing drivers or must have decided that their local regulations did allow. This option was the forerunner of the off-road optional exhaust which would be offered for the following seven years.

ELECTRICS

Other than points described in 'Engines', there were no significant changes to electrical systems for the 1961 and '62 model years.

ENGINE IDENTIFICATION

Engine block cast numbers

1961	283cu in (V8)	3756519 or 3789935
1962	327cu in (V8)	3782870

Stamped engine number suffixes

1961	283cu in (V8)	CQ	230bhp 1x4B carb manual
	283cu in (V8)	DG	230bhp 1x4B carb auto
	283cu in (V8)	CT	245bhp 2x4B carb manual
	283cu in (V8)	DJ	245bhp 2x4B carb auto
	283cu in (V8)	CR	275bhp injection manual
	283cu in (V8)	CU	270bhp 2x4B carb manual
	283cu in (V8)	CS	315bhp injection high-lift cam manual
1962	327cu in (V8)	RC	250bhp WCFB 4B carb manual
	327cu in (V8)	SC	250bhp WCFB 4B carb auto
	327cu in (V8)	RD	300bhp AFB 4B carb manual
	327cu in (V8)	SD	300bhp AFB 4B carb auto
	327cu in (V8)	RE	340bhp AFB 4B carb high-lift cam manual
	327cu in (V8)	RF	360bhp AFB 4B injection high-lift cam manual

Close-up view of 340bhp 327 showing ribbed valve cover and aluminum intake manifold.

TRANSMISSION

Just under a quarter of 1961 buyers decided that the three-speed manual transmission was adequate for their needs. Two-thirds paid extra for the four-speed and the rest bought the automatic.

The standard transmission for '61 and '62 remained the cast iron three-speed Saginaw, with main case cast number 3743368; the tail housing cast number changed to 3787067. Internally the gear ratios were

Wheel variations. Narrow whitewall tire is seen on black-painted '62 wheel, with stock full hubcap. Optional 5.5in wide wheels were supplied with small Chevrolet passenger car hubcaps because these wheels lacked the tags for the full hubcaps, and presumably because their trims looked more sporty.

wider because the close-ratio Saginaw – with 2.21:1 first gear – that had been used previously was discontinued, and the standard ratio as used in passenger cars was adopted.

First gear ratio was 2.47:1, second was 1.53:1 and top, as usual, was direct. A lower first gear permits a taller (numerically lower) rear axle ratio and this was offered for the first time in 1961 in the form of a 3.36:1 as the standard ratio. This ratio was not available with four-speed or automatic transmissions in '61, but became standard with them on arrival of the more powerful 327 engine in '62.

A 3.08:1 axle (RPO 203) became available for the first time with the 327 in '62; prior to this the 283 motor would probably have struggled to handle such a tall ratio under all normal top gear circumstances.

The 3.08 could be ordered as a Positraction axle (see below) under extra-cost RPO 675 or as plain differential under this no-cost RPO 203. To have the 3.08 axle, it was required that the wide-ratio four-speed (see below) and either 250bhp or 300bhp engines were selected. For enjoying fast driving in a '62 on modern roads, this would be a very desirable and perhaps ideal combination.

Some time between mid-November and Christmas 1960, the main cases of the optional T-10 four-speed manual gearbox (RPO 685) installed on '61 Corvettes changed from T10-1B cast iron construction to T10-1C aluminum. This resulted in a weight saving of about 15lbs, and made the task of changing the clutch easier as well. The clutch remained at 10in diameter – more than capable of dealing with as much torque as could be put to the skinny tires before they started to spin.

The four-speed option remained largely unchanged for '62, as did the ratios when ordered with 340bhp and 360bhp motors; with a 2.20:1 first gear, this really was a close-ratio 'box. When ordered with the base 250bhp or 300bhp engines, however, the four-speed was delivered with wide-ratio gears: 2.54:1 first, 1.92:1 second, 1.51:1 third and direct top. These ratio differences for the four-speed may have been indicated by different suffix letters to the option designation – RPO 685A (wide-ratio) or RPO 685B (close-ratio). For '62 the design of the rear case was changed, cast T10-7D instead of the previous T10-7B, and required the use of a different support bracket.

The ultra-reliable cast iron two-speed Powerglide automatic (RPO 313) saw its last year of full use in the Corvette in 1961, but remained for 283-powered cars in '62. Gear ratio in 'drive' was direct, in low and reverse 1.82:1; shift pattern remained L-D-N-R-P, read front to rear.

In '62 the lighter aluminum-cased Powerglide (still RPO 313) was introduced with a revised 1.76:1 low and reverse ratio, and a change to the modern P-R-N-D-L shift pattern – a very important point for driving today. The new aluminum case was very simple compared with the unit it replaced, comprising just a main case and a tail housing instead of five castings bolted together. As with previous Powerglide transmissions in Corvettes, no transmission oil cooler was used.

Usage of the Positraction limited-slip rear axle (RPO 675) jumped from 63 per cent to 98 per cent with the introduction of the more powerful 327 engine, and it is hard to know why. It is partly explained by the fact that all optional ratios were now Positraction only, but why would a clientele who almost all went for whitewall tires also suddenly have the good sense to start choosing a limited slip axle?

Ratios of 3.36, 3.70, 4.11 and 4.56:1 were available in '61 with manual transmissions, but not with the automatic. The following year a 3.08:1 Positraction became available for the wide-ratio four-speed (RPO

685A), and Positraction was also available at last for the two-speed Powerglide in a 3.36:1 ratio only.

WHEELS & TIRES

Wheels and full wheel covers continued as before, and for both years the wheel color was the same as the body color. However, for 1962 black wheels were supplied if whitewall tires were specified.

Wide 15in×5.5in wheels with small hubcaps (RPO 276) were continuously offered from 1957 through '62, but this option was never taken up by more than 4.5 per cent of buyers, even though it was free. These wheels permitted larger 7.10/7.60×15 tires to be fitted, although cars with wide wheels were delivered with the standard 6.70×15 tires. It was not until the mid-1960s that wide wheels came to be considered stylish and became fashionable. In both years wide wheels were painted body color, while the hubcaps were unchanged from 1960.

Whitewall tires (RPO290) came in the same 6.70×15 size as the blackwalls and cost an extra $31.55 for five. In 1961 this option was even more popular than the heater, with 90 per cent of buyers (10 per cent more than in '57) opting for appearance before performance. In '62 a narrower ⅞in whitewall band replaced the previous year's 2½in band. A widely used GM publicity picture of a '57 Corvette next to a Cessna airplane showed the car fitted with narrow-band whitewalls, but these were never fitted by the factory until '62.

SUSPENSION & STEERING

Suspension and steering continued unchanged for the 1961 and '62 model years.

BRAKES

The standard drum brakes continued as before, but there were two brake options.

With the Heavy Duty Brakes & Suspension option (RPO 687), the 1961 facelift did not affect the ducting from the outer grille openings to the rear body – the principle feature of this racing-only option. Optional metallic brakes (RPO 686), with their segmented, sintered-metallic, bonded linings, were also unchanged from 1960, but adopted by many more buyers. For these years they were promoted for their water and fade resistance. Unlike the brakes available under RPO 687, these did not have ventilated backing plates or finned drums.

OPTIONS

Many options have been discussed through this chapter, but the full list of options available for the 1961 and '62 model years is given in the panel.

Elephant's ear front brake cooling scoop as used on '60-62 models with the Heavy Duty Brakes & Suspension option; brake drum is finned for cooling. It was intended that these ears should be fitted prior to a race and removed before the car was used again on the street. The factory left them in the trunk for the owner to fit.

OPTIONS

1961

Code	Option	Quantity	Price
–	Corvette convertible	10939	$3934.00
Standard	283/230hp motor	5357	No cost
FOA 101	Heater	10671	$102.25
FOA 102	Wonder Bar radio	9316	$137.75
RPO 276	15x5.5in wheels	337	No cost
RPO 290	6.70x15 whitewall tires	9780	$31.55
RPO 313	Powerglide automatic	1458	$199.10
RPO 353	275hp fuel injection motor	118	$484.20
RPO 354	315hp fuel injection motor	1462	$484.20
RPO 419	Auxiliary hard-top	5680	$236.75
RPO 426	Power windows	698	$59.20
RPO 440	Two-tone paint	3368	$16.15
RPO 468	270bhp 2x4B carb motor	2827	$182.95
RPO 469	245bhp 2x4B carb motor	1175	$150.65
RPO 470	White convertible top	5602	No cost
RPO 473	Power convertible top	422	$161.40
RPO 675	Positraction axle	6915	$43.05
RPO 685	Four-speed T-10 transmission	7013	$188.30
RPO 686	Metallic brakes	1402	$37.30
RPO 687	Heavy Duty Brakes & Suspension	233	$333.60
LPO 1408	6.70x15 nylon tires	–	$15.75
LPO 1625	24-gallon fuel tank	–	$161.40

1962

Code	Option	Quantity	Price
–	Corvette Convertible	14531	$4038.00
Standard	327/250bhp motor	4907	No cost
FOA 102	Wonder Bar radio	13076	$137.75
RPO 203	3.08:1 standard axle	–	No cost
RPO 242	PCV for California	–	$5.40
RPO 276	15x5.5in wheels	561	No cost
RPO 313	Powerglide automatic	1532	$199.10
RPO 396	340bhp motor	4412	$107.60
RPO 419	Auxiliary hard-top	8074	$236.75
RPO 426	Power windows	995	$59.20
RPO 470	White convertible top	6625	No cost
RPO 473	Power convertible top	350	$139.90
RPO 488	24-gallon fuel tank	65	$118.40
RPO 582	360bhp fuel injection motor	1918	$484.20
RPO 583	300bhp motor	3294	$53.80
RPO 675	Positraction xxle	14232	$43.05
RPO 685	Four-speed T-10 transmission	11318	$188.30
RPO 686	Metallic brakes	2799	$37.30
RPO 687	Heavy Duty Brakes & Suspension	246	$333.60
LPO 1832	6.70x15 whitewall tires	–	$31.55
LPO 1833	6.70x15 nylon blackwall tires	–	$15.70

STRAIGHT-AXLES TODAY

Today, enthusiasm for the ten years of straight-axle Corvette production is probably greater than it has ever been before. Any correct car that is original or well-restored is worth about the same as a new Corvette, and does not depreciate. These cars are still fun to drive, cheap to run and the envy of all those who smile and wave.

It was not always so. Early on, the first Flint-built '53 models were often sold as '54s to make them seem newer and more desirable. This was easy when frame numbers meant nothing to most buyers, when the serial number was fastened to the hinge pillar with nothing more than two screws and a dab of resin, and cars were often titled under their engine numbers. For years the '54s were the cheapest of all Corvettes.

Many six-cylinder Corvettes were improved – or spoiled if that is your view point – by converting them to V8 power. And when a '55 V8 started to rattle, any good mechanic would have advised the owner to replace the motor with a newer one with a few more cubic inches and provision for an oil filter. Encouraged by *Corvette News,* many '56s and early '57s with original three-speeds quickly collected the new four-speed when it arrived in mid-1957, and a complete kit to do the job was available from Chevrolet dealers everywhere. Even today, it is a bold owner who will take out his four-speed and return his car to iron-cased three-speed for the sake of originality.

Fuel injection systems, first seen in mid-1957, were fine in the hands of their original owners, who would habitually have them serviced by Chevrolet dealers. When the fuelies became used cars, however, they were then maintained by owners or gas stations, who had neither the time nor patience to learn about this new technology, or the desire to know about even fuel mixture distribution between cylinders. If the four-barrel carburetor was good enough for everyone else, why not throw out the injection unit? Luckily most units were not scrapped but hoarded under work benches along with brake drums that were too bad to skim but too good to discard.

Fortunately, the ability of an owner to remove the good original stuff from his 'Vette is exceeded only by his inability to discard it or pass it on to the next owner. Some of the best stories in *Corvette Restorer* (the National Corvette Restorers' Society journal) concern members tracing the very first owners of their cars and discovering that they still have the original jack under the bench and the spare keys in the bottom drawer in the kitchen!

By the time the 1958-60 models were becoming affordable used cars, steel wheels and hubcaps were considered an offence against nature, and they were universally replaced by often heavier but apparently lightweight slotted or dished custom wheels, whose wider tires required air shocks to jack up the tail of the car and a trip to the body shop to enlarge the wheel openings. The hubcaps joined the injection units and brake drums under the bench. The old wheels were too big to fit in the trunk to take home and joined the scrap metal pile at the tire shop.

Tubular exhaust headers have always been a high-profit/low-benefit item, and have been sold to innocent owners with the familiar false claims of more power, better economy and eternal vigor. By the time that the weekly replacement of header flange gaskets became boring, and the pinging noise infuriating, it was too late. The front down-pipes had been cut off and the ram's horn manifolds had gone for scrap too.

Rust does not bother Corvettes like it does other cars, but as the 1958-60 tail pipes rusted away unseen, so would the acidic exhaust gases attack the fine rear bumpers that shrouded them. Those that were fitted with Thrush or Hooker side exhausts at least saved their back bumpers, but probably discarded their original exhaust manifolds in favor of headers too.

From 1960 the high-performance Corvettes – and from early '61 all models – had nice Harrison Division of General Motors aluminum radiators. Unlike the copper units they replaced, they needed anti-freeze to inhibit corrosion. Not a problem in the snow belt, but in the hot south and west, where city water was all that most cooling systems ever tasted, the aluminum radiators quickly rotted from the inside.

During the mid-1970s, the customizing craze diminished and a few people started to return cars to stock condition, but then a new money spinner – in-car entertainment – arrived. Now any car had to have a sound system and the Corvette needed the most powerful. Many a custom wheel shop became a stereo specialist overnight, and a tire fitter whose wife would not trust him to change a fuse at home was delving behind the precious instrument panel to install rat nests of wiring, to connect an 8-Track tape player and two big speakers. These required big holes to be chopped with a sabre saw, and wiring, often with fuses omitted for simplicity, sometimes caused small electrical fires that on occasion grew into larger fires.

Add to all this the inevitable major and minor scrapes and wrecks, conversions into drag and circuit race cars (remember that preparing a Corvette for racing can do more damage to an original car in five hours than a careless owner can do in five years) and wonder what is left from the original pool of 69,000 '53-62 Corvettes.

Ed Cole's fiberglass dream car has survived all this and returned as the most popular classic car for the very best of reasons. Firstly, it looks great. The body styling of the Motorama car was dramatically ahead of its time in 1953. It was smooth and clean, with faired headlamps, the first wraparound windshield, and a low and wide stance. Then there is that curving and diving hoop of chrome that defines the cockpit, starting and ending at the seat divider, looping behind each seat, along the door tops and over the windshield. Ten years later the '62 looked old-fashioned but still distinguished when compared to the Jaguar XKE, and retired from the fray to let the Sting Ray carry on waving the crossed flag of Chevrolet and the chequered flag of the finish line.

The early Corvette has become an American icon, along with the '59 Cadillac, the Harley Davidson and the colonnaded colonial home. It has become evocative background furniture to sell a thousand consumer products, from beer to perfume. It has become more desirable just by being in the background of so many TV and press advertisements. The process started in Bert Leonard's and Stirling Silliphant's *Route 66* TV series, which used Corvettes supplied free of charge by Chevrolet, and has not stopped since.

The fiberglass body has cancelled the corrosion effect that has been the death of so many steel-bodied cars. Unless fire-damaged, a Corvette can rarely be totalled, and the thick die-formed fiberglass bodywork does not even suffer from significant cracking. The frame was made extra strong so that it would not twist and impair the handling, but that made it almost indestructible too. All the moving parts were lifted from heavier passenger cars so that they were rugged to start with and then under-stressed in the Corvette.

General Motors has always run a very efficient parts distribution operation. When even the quietest small town has a Chevrolet dealer, it has always been easy to order parts for the older Corvette. GM was into computerization of its parts system early, and this has helped the tracing of obscure or discontinued parts nationwide when required. With its principal headquarters, General Motors Service Parts Operation, appropriately in Flint, Michigan, and a network of 21 Warehousing and Distribution Centers, overnight or even same-day delivery has always been possible. Usefully the parts system is GM-wide, so that a Pontiac dealer can source Corvette parts just as easily as a Chevrolet dealer if that is more convenient.

Considering the age of straight-axle Corvettes, the number of parts still available from GM is remarkable. Some parts were discontinued very soon after each model year finished production. These were mainly trim items such as door panels, seat upholstery and carpets, and these parts were often the first products of after-market specialists. Other parts would be dropped quickly where a later year item would be a functional replacement in the eyes of an average owner. These would include, for instance, control knobs, mirrors, cylinder heads, air cleaners and exhaust manifolds. The parts that remained available the longest tended to be those used in major overhauls such as engine and axle parts, and crash repair parts like bumpers, body panels, emblems and lamps.

The after-market has developed into a multi-million dollar industry employing thousands. Most of these publish excellent catalogs, and specialise in mail order. If it seems that they are based in obscure locations and do not encourage visitors, it is with good reason. Having been in this business myself for 20 years, I know that customers on the telephone spend their money about five times faster than those who walk in requiring personal service! The owner on the 'phone needs no heat, light or space, and leaves no footprints either, and because he is using a credit card spends more freely. Bear this in mind next time you 'phone for parts...

The parts sold by specialists are still mainly sourced from GM, often re-packaged and re-numbered. When a part starts becoming hard to obtain, the specialists buy up all the stock they can and raise the price, in anticipation of a price hike. Sometimes the demand will trigger a response at Service Parts Operation, who will order the original supplier of the part to clean up the tooling and run some more, to take advantage of the apparent popularity of the part.

Many of the reproduction parts come from a host of small specialists, many working part-time in the evening at home. Corvette restorers need to be practical people, and many have full-time jobs in industries which can make the parts they need. They start out making one piece for themselves at work and end up making hundreds which they sell through small advertisements or direct to the big catalog vendors.

The fiberglass body panels on the St Louis built 1954-62 models were of excellent quality, but when damaged they were often replaced by cheaper hand-laid panels with the characteristic hairy inside finish, many of the original GM matched-die panels having been discontinued too. Now more of the matched-die panels are being reproduced.

The restorer who wants to rebuild his car for show and to be judged can be starting up a very long and expensive path, but the satisfaction can be immeasurable. Restoration of fine things as a hobby is not confined to automobiles, and cars are arguably the most important art works of the 20th Century. There can be no doubt that the most intensely designed artefact that most Americans will see on any day will be an automobile, a point not lost on the Museum of Modern Art when they organised an exhibition of the finest modern cars in 1951, unfortunately too late for the Corvette to be featured, or worse excluded.

The urge to restore something neglected into something beautiful runs deep, and costs tend to be forgotten when elusive parts are sought. As so many parts have dates cast or stamped into them, a correct car must bear not only the right cast numbers, but build dates that precede the assembly date by a reasonable number of weeks or months. Such parts can be scarce. And once you have found and fitted a pair of correct 3725563 two-hole flange exhaust manifolds to your '56, are you ever again going to risk cracking that expensive old cast iron by driving the car hard?

A good straight-axle restoration today should include correct factory style paint and crayon markings on the frame, but once these are on who would risk dirtying them by using the car to drive to work? The aim of the perfect restoration is to put the car back to the condition it was in at the moment it was driven out of the back doors at St Louis to await ship-

Views of an original and unrestored 1960 290bhp fuelie in daily use. Underside of engine shows a few oil leaks, and oil filter has been converted to modern spin-on type. Rear shows mid-placement of mufflers and rear sway bar introduced in 1960.

ment by Complete Auto Transit Inc. It has to be that moment, because after a week outside in industrial St Louis the state of the car can be imagined!

The NCRS is widely perceived as having encouraged the perfectly restored, trailered and never-driven Corvette. While this is undoubtedly true, the NCRS has done much to put this right, and the majority of its members certainly do not own 'trailer queens'. In its judging manuals it is clearly stated that there can be no deduction of marks 'for modest amounts of dust, oil, and road dirt, as NCRS encourages the driving of these vehicles'.

Performance Verification is another goal to aim for and a prerequisite for the Duntov Mark of Excellence Award. The car is started from cold and must perform to manufacturer's specifications, including maximum acceleration, on a five-mile or longer road course, and every item must function perfectly. Points up to 10 per cent of the total score are also awarded if the car is driven more than 100 miles to a judging meet, although the first 100 miles do not count at all. The NCRS also runs great Road Tours where a participant's road mileage can add to the car's total score.

My impression of the NCRS is that its members and officials combine extraordinary knowledge and love of the Corvette. Many countries now have draconian restrictions on the use of older cars, but so far the US has lost only its leaded gasoline. There are very few, if any, car enthusiasts on Capitol Hill, and the NCRS may yet find itself fighting to keep on the road

cars that are perceived as gas-guzzling polluters. If early Corvette owners are seen to be happy to trailer their cars, this will not help our case at all.

In Europe, a Corvette on a trailer will elicit sympathy for the obvious and shameful mechanical failure, or derisive laughter from Jaguar, Porsche and Ferrari owners. This is really how it should be, even allowing for the vast distances and interstate highways in the US, where it is no harder to tow a car on a trailer than to drive it. It is a shame that the judging standard is 'assembly plant despatch area fresh' and not '10,000 miles and 12 months of careful ownership from new', even if the latter would be harder to judge.

Presently there has been little attempt to apply modern emission standards to these cars. If we are forced to comply then at least we have the easiest car to convert. Do not tell the EPA, but just a day's work will fit a modern 1985-86 Tuned Port Corvette injection unit and intake to any 1955-62 V8, using existing bolt holes and standard gaskets. An oxygen sensor and boss go into one downpipe, and a few hundred dollars will buy an ECM and wiring harness. A high-pressure fuel pump with an additional return pipe are also required. A positive crankcase ventilation system must be connected, easier if the heads are changed too, along with a pair of catalytic converters in the exhaust to complete an environmental package, which will be more economical, better starting and offer considerably more torque.

Unfortunately, it will not be original.

ACKNOWLEDGEMENTS

With many thanks to Mark Hughes of Bay View Books for his patience and encouragement, and to James Mann for his excellent photographs. Special thanks are due to the members of the Mason Dixon Chapter of the National Corvette Restorers' Society who allowed their cars to be photographed and gave freely of their time, in particular Tony Avedisian, Chuck Berge, Chuck Gongloff, Udo Horn, Steve Lesser, Don Loveless, Carl Markert, Jay Matricciani, Dennis Moore, Jim Moran, Fred Mullauer, Mike Shepard, Steve Sokoloff, Doug Sonders and Tony Zagorski, and their friends – and also Bill Herron. I also thank the authors of each of the works itemised below in the bibliography; one cannot write a book on such an already well-researched subject without reading and comparing their work first. Finally, thanks to Charles Herridge of Bay View Books who, unusually in his trade, believes that corrections must be incorporated each time one of his books is reprinted. I thank you, the reader, in advance for your comments and corrections, which should be sent to the publisher or e-mailed to me, Tom Falconer, at ClaremontC@aol.com.

BIBLIOGRAPHY

There has been an extraordinary number of books covering the Chevrolet Corvette, more possibly than about any other car. They vary from the colorful and inaccurate to works of intense research and dry but unimpeachable fact. I have consulted all of those mentioned below, many of which are indispensable to the owner of a straight-axle Corvette. They are listed broadly in order of excellence.

Corvette: America's Star Spangled Sports Car by Karl Ludvigsen, 1973 (Automobile Quarterly). This is the first and still the outstanding narrative work, particularly on the early history, by an author who worked at GM and knew many of the participants.

The Complete Corvette Restoration and Technical Guide – Volume 1, 1953 through 1962 by Noland Adams, 1980 (Automobile Quarterly). With 432 pages of properly researched, checked and accurate fact, this is the indisputable encyclopaedic work on the 1953-62 models. Anyone with one of these cars *must* have this book. I freely acknowledge that this book was open on my desk throughout my own endeavors.

The Best of Corvette News 1957-76 edited by Karl Ludvigsen, 1976 (Automobile Quarterly). This work contains 656 pages of superb articles about the Corvette from Chevrolet's own free magazine. Excellent technical features written without the benefit of hindsight, and full of the flavor of the era.

Corvette, American Legend, Vol 1: The Beginning by Noland Adams, 1996 (Cars and Parts Magazine). The author's outstanding photographic collection put together with fascinating captions. This first volume has 250 pages and only covers the story to the end of 1953, before production started at St Louis.

Corvette Judging Manuals 1953-55, 1956-57, 1958-60, 1961-62 by various authors (National Corvette Restorers' Society). Excellent reference and the final arbiter if your Corvette is being judged for an NCRS award. The perfect guide to cast and stamped part numbers and original finishes on visible parts for a restored car, based on the widest available information from members of the largest club. Contrary to popular myth, NCRS members do drive their cars too!

Chevrolet by the Numbers 1955-59 and *1960-64* by Alan L. Colvin, 1996 (Robert Bentley). The first two volumes of a four-volume series. Fascinating, erudite, correct and beautifully produced, these are outstanding academic works and compulsive reading. As well as the major engine and transmission parts, Colvin covers crankshafts, camshafts and rear axles, and much more that is hard to find elsewhere. He sensibly concentrates on cast numbers, not the now irrelevant part numbers.

Corvette: An American Legend, Volume 1 1953-67 by Roy D. Query, 1986 (Automobile Quarterly). Superb color photography of certified Bloomington Gold cars, with good narrative text. The detailed pictures are good enough to guide the restorer, and encourage the rest.

Corvette, Sports Car of America by M.B. Antonick, 1980 (Michael Bruce Associates). This book contains an excellent and lengthy illustrated feature on the 1953-55 models by John Amgwert, editor of the NCRS Corvette Restorer Magazine.

Corvette Black Book, 1953-97 by M.B. Antonick, 1997 (Michael Bruce Associates). All the information you could need in a pocket-sized format. First published in 1978 and now in its 12th edition. Indispensable.

1953-1972 Corvette Pocket Spec Guide by John Amgwert, 1991 (National Corvette Restorers' Society). Pocket-sized and spiral-bound, this is the book you take to flea markets. It lists all the important cast numbered and dated components by category, then by year. Faced with a pile of starter motors and intake manifolds, you could select all the Corvette ones in minutes. All the early *Corvette Black Book* information and more.

The Corvette Plastic Body by E.J. Premo, 1954 (Society of Automotive Engineers). Prepared as a paper by the Chevrolet Engineering Department and presented to the Society at their Annual Meeting by body man Jim Premo, this is a fascinating account of the state in reinforced plastics in 1953 and how Chevrolet approached its use.

Corvette Service Operations – Chassis (General Motors Corporation). Published in 1960 and widely available in reprint, this book dates from an era when GM cared about what it published. Written in beautifully concise English and superbly illustrated, it contains the definitive guide to fuel injection. Makes you want to tune up your car right now, just like a good cook book sends you to the kitchen. Compare this to any GM manual post-1981, date of the first ECM, and weep.

Corvette Servicing Guide (General Motors Corporation). Published 1962 and still available. This is the shop manual for 1953-62 Corvettes and needs to be read in conjunction with the appropriate year of Passenger Car manual.

Cadillac, The Complete History by Maurice D. Hendry, 1979 (Automobile Quarterly). You cannot be deeply into Corvettes without being drawn into the other GM Divisions – the cross-fertilization inherent in the GM career structure made the Corvette what it is. Harley Earl, Ed Cole, Bill Mitchell, Maurice Olley, Harry Barr and current Corvette chief engineer Dave Hill all started out or spent much of their careers with Cadillac.